Teaching Shakespeare With Purpose

RELATED TITLES AVAILABLE FROM BLOOMSBURY
ARDEN SHAKESPEARE:

Creative Shakespeare: The Globe Education Guide to Practical Shakespeare, Fiona Banks
Essential Shakespeare: The Arden Guide to Text and Interpretation, Pamela Bickley and Jenny Stevens
Shakespeare for Young People: Productions, Versions and Adaptations, Abigail Rokison
Transforming the Teaching of Shakespeare With the Royal Shakespeare Company, Joe Winston

Teaching Shakespeare with Purpose

A Student-Centred Approach

Ayanna Thompson
and
Laura Turchi

THE ARDEN SHAKESPEARE
LONDON • NEW YORK • OXFORD • NEW DELHI • SYDNEY

THE ARDEN SHAKESPEARE
Bloomsbury Publishing Plc
50 Bedford Square, London, WC1B 3DP, UK

BLOOMSBURY, THE ARDEN SHAKESPEARE and the
Arden Shakespeare logo are trademarks of Bloomsbury Publishing Plc

First published in Great Britain 2016
Reprinted 2016, 2017, 2018

© Ayanna Thompson and Laura Turchi, 2016

Ayanna Thompson and Laura Turchi have asserted their right under the Copyright, Designs
and Patents Act, 1988, to be identified as author of this work.

For legal purposes the Acknowledgements on p. viii constitute an
extension of this copyright page.

All rights reserved. No part of this publication may be reproduced or transmitted in any
form or by any means, electronic or mechanical, including photocopying, recording, or
any information storage or retrieval system, without prior permission in writing from the
publishers.

Bloomsbury Publishing Plc does not have any control over, or responsibility for,
any third-party websites referred to or in this book. All internet addresses given in this
book were correct at the time of going to press. The author and publisher regret
any inconvenience caused if addresses have changed or sites have ceased to exist,
but can accept no responsibility for any such changes.

No responsibility for loss caused to any individual or organization acting on or refraining
from action as a result of the material in this publication can be accepted by Bloomsbury or
the author.

A catalogue record for this book is available from the British Library.

ISBN: HB: 978-1-4725-9962-9
PB: 978-1-4725-9961-2
ePDF: 978-1-4725-9964-3
ePub: 978-1-4725-9963-6

A catalog record for this book is available from the Library of Congress.

Typeset by Fakenham Prepress Solutions, Fakenham, Norfolk NR21 8NN

Printed and bound in Great Britain

To find out more about our authors and books visit
www.bloomsbury.com and sign up for our newsletters.

CONTENTS

LIST OF ILLUSTRATIONS

ACKNOWLEDGEMENTS

We would like to dedicate this book to Peggy O'Brien and Margaret Bartley for their steadfast commitment to this project and unstinting enthusiasm for our collaboration.

Ayanna would like to thank her colleagues at GW, who have had sustained conversations with her about pedagogy, Jeffrey Cohen and Holly Dugan. Who could ask for better? She would also like to thank Derek, Dashiell and Thaisa for their love and support. Much love!

Laura would like to express her admiration for the strong women who grounded her own teacher education, especially Sandy Fallon, Lorana Gleason and Bobbi Helling; her appreciation for the hospitality of Lynne Warham and her colleagues at Edge Hill University; and her abiding love for Pete and Reed.

N.B.: All citations from William Shakespeare come for the Arden editions of his plays.

1

The realities of the twenty-first century

There has been an explosion in resources for teachers who want to introduce young school children (primary/elementary students) to William Shakespeare's works.[1] While there are individual teachers and authors who have written useful essays and books (e.g. Abigail Rokison, Brian Edmiston and Rafe Esquith[2]), there are also well-established educational outreach programmes run by theatre companies whose curricula specifically focus on young school children (e.g. The Globe, Royal Shakespeare Company and the Chicago Shakespeare Company). These resources support performance-based activities and/or rehearsal-room processes in order to energize Shakespeare from page to stage. The goal of these resources is to empower teachers to head-off fears of Shakespeare by exploring the works through play; they work through active, imaginative and collaborative approaches. At the end of these units, students are expected to have developed a universal appreciation for Shakespeare, which is no easy task for many 7–14 year olds.

What is the next stage for the educators of 15–20 year olds? The programs for young students inspire us to ask: how can educators move their students from appreciation to independent facility with complex texts? If those students have an appreciation for Shakespeare, how can we build their skills in reading, writing, speaking, listening, viewing and creating when they are advanced learners? How can we combine the pleasure of socially collaborative activities with heightened expectations for individual critical analysis? As we acknowledge our 15–20 year olds' developing interests in diverse identity politics (race, gender, sexuality, physical ability), does this affect our Shakespeare units? Which twenty-first-century digital texts and/or tools will our students find compelling, stimulating and actually useful (as opposed to distracting and addictive)?

---

[1]Because we are addressing UK and US teachers, we have employed a hybrid terminology throughout. When we write about primary/elementary students, we mean children ages 7–14.
[2]Rokison, *Shakespeare for Young People*; Edmiston, *Transforming Teaching and Learning with Active and Dramatic Approaches*; and Esquith, *There Are No Shortcuts*.

A typical active approach to Shakespeare in which students learn through embodying the roles. This image comes from the Braeburn International School's (Tanzania) study of Othello. *By kind permission of Braeburn International School Arusha.*

Teaching Shakespeare with Purpose provides a bridge for students from appreciation to analysis without disavowing the fun. After all, learning to analyse a complex text is pleasurable, like working through any difficult puzzle. Secondary teachers who envy the play time of younger grade levels, and who recognize the value of active approaches, will find resources here for advanced learners. Theatre-based classroom techniques that allow students to discover meaning in a speech or a scene, however, are only one dimension of the active approaches appropriate for advanced learners. In order to advance literacy at this level there are editions, performances, critical lenses and media to compare. Our approach to active learning is inclusive of, but not restricted to, performance-based pedagogies. The recently coined US phrase 'college and career readiness' describes a vital developmental stage in which students gain facility with complex texts. We use the term *advanced learners* to describe the students who are the focus of this book. They are advanced in school age; we expect that they vary widely in ability and motivation to understand Shakespeare's plays on their own. In order for advanced learners to be university and employment ready they need to be collaboratively and independently engaged in complex texts. This book shows how.

Teaching Shakespeare with Purpose is unique in its attempt to speak to both secondary and collegiate educators in the UK and the US. Literature instructors at the secondary level, with students of all abilities, will be given the tools to reimagine their Shakespeare units with an eye towards goals and purposes. Instructors who teach Advanced Placement courses in literature (in the US), A-level courses in literature (in the UK) or International Baccalaureate courses (anywhere) will also benefit from these new activities for deeply engaged reading, debate, performance and investigation. At the collegiate level, instructors who teach introductory Shakespeare courses will be given strategies to expand their pedagogical repertoire.

We recognize that addressing the education of diverse 15–20 year olds is unusual: this is not an age range that is recognized by institutional divisions. Nonetheless, we take seriously the importance of and necessity for college and career readiness for advanced learners. A facility with complex texts, of course, is necessary for success in the twenty-first century (for the individual and for society). While many schools in the UK and the US have acquired twenty-first-century hardware and software, their pedagogies still remain firmly rooted in the twentieth century. Despite the fact that Shakespeare is 450 years old, we deliver a twenty-first-century pedagogy through him and his plays.

Twenty-first-century learning

Who are the students in our classrooms? The age group (15–20 years old) we have identified intentionally crosses standard institutional groupings in both the UK and the US. But we also want to recognize that these advanced learners have specific twenty-first-century habits for knowledge acquisition and enactment. Their learning habits arise from the technological tools that have made digital information and connectivity the norm.

As we will discuss further in Chapter 4, there has been substantial media coverage speculating about 'Millennials' and research conducted about them for marketing, political and social reasons. Given the pace of technological change in the UK and the US, it is not surprising that educators are trying to understand the impact of new tools and connectivity on students. Teachers, classrooms and schools have different levels of success in harnessing the new learning habits toward traditional or scholarly aims.

Our thinking about advanced learners and Shakespeare has been shaped by researchers studying New Media Literacies, notably the work of Henry Jenkins and James Paul Gee.[3] The challenge is to understand

---

[3]For examples of twenty-first-century learning habits, see Jenkins et al., *Confronting the Challenges of Participatory Culture: Media Education for the 21st Century*; and Gee, *What Video Games Have to Teach Us About Learning and Literacy*.

the correspondences and disconnections between formal education processes and the habits formed outside of school: for instance, strategies that arise from learning to navigate social media, multiplayer games and ever-evolving handheld devices. The Shakespeare activities we present in this book are inspired by four specific habits of learning that twenty-first-century advanced learners value:

- Participation in informal learning communities.
- Explicit explorations of identity.
- Following divergent paths to knowledge.
- Innovative performances of their knowledge.

By *informal learning communities* we of course mean collaborative groups of students, which are not unusual in classrooms. Our emphasis, however, is on how these groups can mirror James Gee's affinity groups, or Henry Jenkins's participatory culture, but in the admittedly artificial context of a classroom.[4] Think of the wikis (an online information platform, a website collaboratively edited by other players) that offer winning strategies for the gamer. How does participatory culture look – how do informal learning communities function – in a Shakespeare classroom? The activities we offer, which use specific passages from different Shakespeare plays, assume that the teacher knows her classroom and the kinds of small communities that she can create and manage. Advanced learners need opportunities to make meaning together, combining their insights and pooling their understanding. This work may be face-to-face in the classroom or mediated beyond it, but the goal is to crowdsource understanding rather than to isolate students in their struggle with complex texts.

There is no reason to pretend that informal learning groups arise naturally (especially at the beginning of a unit) because the students are eager to delve into a complex text. But the teacher's design for collaboration can mean that the difficulties are surmountable, the puzzle-solving is pleasurable (especially in the context of collaboration) and what is discovered about Shakespeare's plays is meaningful and has value to twenty-first-century learners.

What is the teacher's role? Master teacher Mark Miazga of Baltimore, Maryland describes setting student activities into motion and coaching them to explore texts together. Then his instruction comes up 'behind'

---

[4]For *affinity groups,* see Gee, 'Affinity Spaces: From Age of Mythology to Today's Schools'; for *participatory culture,* see Jenkins, 'Confronting the Challenges of Participatory Culture: Media Education for the 21st Century (Part One)'.

the students to focus them on aspects of a scene or act that they may have missed.[5] As further chapters will demonstrate, the complexity of Shakespeare's texts will probably require explicit teaching of new skills – most importantly, the teacher modelling the moves of close reading. The teacher is not just standing by waiting to see what will happen.

Another twenty-first-century habit of learning is the *explicit exploration of identity*. This is not to suggest that such exploration is easy, just that it is a natural extension of the connected world in which we live (any scan of the 'comments' section responding to a piece of news offers a quick demonstration of the diversity of identities on display). The work of Brendesha M. Tynes and Suzanne L. Markoe, for instance, explores the contested creation of profiles for social media spaces.[6] As we discuss in Chapter 4, studies of advanced learners reveal that they are in fact confused about racism and bias and eager to have open and respectful discussions about them. Yet current approaches to Shakespeare often segregate his works from intentional discussions of difference (race, gender, ability and/or sexuality) and bias. The more culturally responsive approach we promote recognizes that students bring their own perspectives and identities to their experience of Shakespeare's plays – just as audiences have for more than 400 years. The global awareness that is made possible by internet connectivity is an asset in the Shakespeare classroom because it emphasizes that there are always multiple and varied interpretive viewpoints.

Shakespeare's plays are so well established in the canon and curriculum that one may assume that acts of inquiry are only possible in the most rarefied research settings. Instead, our focus on *divergent paths to knowledge* as a twenty-first-century learning habit builds on the reality that our students have always had the internet and they expect to find answers through surfing. The marvellous complexity of a Shakespeare play offers students many starting places for exploration and discovery, grounded in the text and with resonances in literary, historical, contemporary, cultural, political and artistic worlds at least. A Shakespeare classroom should be built on the expectation that students' ideas matter, that the ideas that a group collectively generates are valuable and that searching for plausible explanations or illuminating details always leads to new questions as well as new insights to a text. Our suggested exercises focus students on ideas to be explored in the text as they develop increased facility and independent thinking beyond simply completing an assignment 'for' the teacher. Such a stance of learning

---

[5] Miazga, 'Shakespeare and the (Common Core) Assessments'.
[6] Tynes and Markoe, 'The Role of Color-Blind Racial Attitudes in Reactions to Racial Discrimination on Social Network Sites'.

through inquiry incorporates what Chris Dede and others have called 'know[ing] how to keep learning'.[7]

Finally, we recognize the twenty-first-century learner's preference for creating *innovative performances of knowledge*, and the wide-ranging digital tools – for drafting, as well as 'final' presentations – that can be available. Henry Jenkins' description of collaborative authorship within participatory cultures offers a useful parallel to the context of early modern acting companies in which Shakespeare's plays first appeared. For instance twenty-first-century advanced learners recognize how the creation of fan fiction requires deep if sometimes contested understanding of a particular text. To what extent are the endlessly new and creative expressions possible in a Shakespeare classroom? We note the potential constraints of sufficient connectivity and available digital tools, but encourage Shakespeare teachers to recognize that performing one's understanding well requires identifying rigorous correspondences between a complex text and its contemporary (for instance) adaptation. Not all classrooms or schools are prepared to support twenty-first-century learning, but Shakespeare classrooms can include assignments that press students to demonstrate their learning in ways that expand and enrich the traditional essay or enactment of a scene.

For too many young adults there are two distinct Shakespeares: one that sizzles as the latest production, adaptation, meme or parody emerges online, on the big screen or in print; and the other from school – the toughest slog with language to be translated, endless footnotes to be consulted and historical trivia to be regurgitated. Even if students are doing more than shallow Shakespeare, they are likely receiving a predigested, prescribed and limited Shakespeare. This is a lost opportunity not only for enjoying the plays, but also for developing critical skills. Shakespeare sits at the centre of this book because his works are the mother lode of complex texts. Where better than to develop a facility with complex texts than with the author who has remained at the wellspring of literary studies?

We have observed classrooms in which Shakespeare study is defined by factoid recall, character identification and plot summaries (e.g. a completed study guide = mastery of *Romeo and Juliet*). We have also observed more advanced students who are required to swallow whole the teacher's carefully constructed interpretation of Shakespeare. Despite the best content and delivery, this approach still renders knowledge acquisition as a passive endeavour: the students are only expected to regurgitate (e.g. essay assignment = rephrase the teacher). We have also observed teachers

---

[7]Dede, 'Comparing Frameworks for 21st Century Skills', 57.

who espouse the value of exploratory learning by using the internet. Nonetheless, many of these assignments end up resembling scavenger hunts rather than purposeful explorations (e.g. Webquest = who was Julius Caesar).

While there is a renewed interest in performance-based approaches (especially in primary/elementary schools), these approaches do not take full advantage of what twenty-first-century learning can do for advanced students. Our society needs students who are comfortable, skilled and find enjoyment in wrestling, contending and creating their own complex texts. So for the secondary school and the introductory university teaching of Shakespeare we offer a new Shakespeare curriculum, one that is intentional and responsive.

Many educators (and the specialists who write about them) struggle to balance teacher guidance and student freedom, or order and chaos, especially in diverse classrooms. We advocate the creation of frames so that students discover and explore multiple Shakespeares, as texts, performances, history and cultural artefacts. As a result, students are empowered to participate with complex text as readers, writers, speakers, listeners and viewers in the world beyond their classroom. Without a twenty-first-century approach, Shakespeare in schools really will cease to matter – it will be a dead subject like Latin – and will be replaced by texts that are 'relevant' and easily accessible, like *The Hunger Games*. This is not meant to denigrate ancient languages or young adult literature, but to recognize the value in continuing to explore and challenge the relevance of Shakespeare's works. This is a contest that warrants a collective adventure in the Shakespeare classroom.

The purpose of teaching Shakespeare's plays is to increase a student's independent facility with complex texts. This may seem reductive because there are so many pleasures in one's discovery of Shakespeare: insults, songs, fights, passion, fairies, blood, transformations, revenge, friendships, intrigue, betrayal and marriages. We also understand that Shakespeare is enjoyed in multiple media and venues (this is from two authors who stood in line at 5.00 am to get *standing room* tickets for *Coriolanus* in London – we love Shakespeare!). But the *teaching* of Shakespeare is a vehicle rather than a destination: advanced learners need increasingly sophisticated literacy skills to face all complex texts.

While we argue that Shakespeare is not the destination, the vehicle is not inconsequential either because his plays are rewarding both intellectually and aesthetically. Please do not mistake the previous sentence for an argument for Shakespeare's universality. Rather, the plays offer moments of historical transcendence alongside moments of maddeningly mundane expressions of racism, sexism, anti-Semitism, etc. (more on this topic below and in Chapters 3, 4 and 5). One can make an argument for Shakespeare's value even if that argument is not couched in claims of universality. It is important to remember, after all, that our twenty-first-century advanced learners value the explicit exploration of identity in its many facets, and these explorations frequently and justly challenge claims of universality (after all, it is fair to ask if all teenage girls should relate to Ophelia, or if all black boys should see themselves in Hamlet).

If Shakespeare is a good vehicle, what does it mean to have a facility with complex texts? Fundamentally, this transferable skill set enables students to read, write, speak, listen and view analytically (as the English literature scholars say) or to utilize higher order thinking skills (in the parlance of social science). Using these skills with dense, knotty and intricate texts, advanced learners discover how to build persuasive arguments based on complex textual evidence. All students need these skills to be prepared for university and employment in the twenty-first century, and Shakespeare is a fun and effective way to acquire these skills.

In many ways we are offering an interdisciplinary Shakespeare, which we are practicing by writing this book. We, as authors, had offices on the same floor, despite our being trained in two different disciplines. Laura, a social scientist who also prepares student teachers, gnashed her teeth after observing a stultifying Shakespeare lesson. Ayanna, a literary and performance scholar, was exasperated by the fact that her PhD students were not taught how to teach Shakespeare. Initially, we planned to co-teach a class on the teaching of Shakespeare, and eventually this blossomed into the book you are reading. As an act of collaborative writing, this book mirrors the process we advocate.

This book offers pedagogical content knowledge: not just instructional strategies, nor just literary theory, but an extended account for combining the specific content of Shakespeare's plays *and* steps for leading students to insightful and articulate ownership of these texts. Much of our writing together has stretched us, requiring us to bridge learning science and Shakespeare scholarship. For Dr Laura Turchi, years of research on secondary school English classrooms and her years in teacher preparation have led to a pedagogical focus on how teachers can strategically deploy their disciplinary knowledge, especially to create and sustain student engagement. For Dr Ayanna Thompson, years of research on critical approaches to Shakespeare have led to her pedagogical focus on how to teach Shakespeare and contemporary culture. We invite you to further our work with experimentation and discoveries in partnership with your students.

So who are you, reading this book? We imagine that you are multiple, varied and international teachers in literature classrooms.

First, this book is designed for the new secondary teacher, someone who may have had a survey course in Shakespeare and who may have kept brilliant notes. Even so it is unlikely that the pedagogy was transparent or an appropriate model for teaching secondary students. In the US, new teachers may have degrees in other fields than literature, and they may feel

intimidated by the Shakespeare content. US teachers describe their preparation to teach Shakespeare as happening almost exclusively ad hoc and
on-the-job, so that they must depend on colleagues or search on their own
to assemble materials and activities for a unit. It is rare that new teachers
have had specific courses in Shakespeare pedagogy, and equally rare that
any professional development is focused on literature teaching, although
more generic and skill-based approaches to complex texts are available. In
the UK, the requirement of Qualified Teacher Status, which is in addition
to the undergraduate study of English, appears to mean that more teachers
have advanced work in English Language Arts pedagogy. The English
emphasis on Shakespeare, given the cultural and heritage focus within the
curriculum, enables more new teachers to arrive at their first assignments
with skills and materials ready to go. At the same time, as our survey of
active approaches in Chapter 4 suggests, the new Shakespeare teacher in
England may be no more comfortable with teaching Shakespeare through
performance exercises than a teacher in the US.

Our second imagined reader is an enthusiastic veteran, one who has
taught Shakespeare's plays well many times over. Our research indicates,
however, that the veteran teacher may struggle with relevancy, as anyone
who teaches Shakespeare to young adults does, and seeks new strategies for
success with advanced twenty-first-century learners. Experienced teachers
of drama may be familiar with the performance-based approaches and
rehearsal-room techniques that we include and critique, but we are offering
something new with regards to race, gender, sexuality and physical ability,
and the teaching of Shakespeare.

Third, this book is designed for English PhD students and instructors of
introductory post-secondary-level Shakespeare courses. Many who teach
in universities have never had course work on pedagogy, and our research
has shown that there are almost no courses on how to teach Shakespeare at
the university level. As a result, these instructors struggle with basic course
design: how many plays to teach, which plays to teach and how to assess
student learning. *Teaching Shakespeare with Purpose* argues that introductory post-secondary Shakespeare courses should be focused on how
advanced learners gain facility with complex texts.

Throughout we assume that teachers value student-centred classrooms.
Yet student-centred is an over-determined term that frequently boils down
to a teacher's dedication to student work and individual progress. Such
dedication is vitally important, but it is not a pedagogy. This book offers
engaged educators opportunities to restructure their roles as teachers of
Shakespeare. Such teachers do not have to be Shakespeare experts, but they
do need to be purposeful facilitators.

Instructional design and
student-centred classrooms

For many of us, especially while preparing to teach a Shakespeare text, designing an instructional unit and imagining a student-centred classroom seems completely contradictory. How can the complex Shakespeare text itself not be the centre, the focus of attention? Student-centredness, however, is not about abandoning students to whatever interests them, leaving Shakespeare's text at the periphery. Instead, we work to connect what students *need* to know to what they *want* to know. We shamelessly toil to convince them that they do, in fact, want to acquire the skills and habits of inquiry that will allow them to understand complex texts like Shakespeare's plays independently.

Part of the design work for student-centred classrooms is in creating both a physical and an emotional environment that promotes and values collaborations. If we value such collaboration, the emotional environment of the classroom needs to be one in which the teacher models listening as well as speaking. There should be an orderliness to discussion that does not depend on rigid turn-taking rules, such as ones in which only the teacher can determine who will speak and what kind of answer will be allowed.

Another promise of student-centred instruction is increased participation and engagement. As we discuss in Chapter 4, we know many teachers utilize active approaches for teaching Shakespeare's plays with the intent of engaging students. We share in the desire to see students on their feet and working with their whole selves (and their classmates) to experience these texts. As our suggested exercises will outline, we work to then provide bridges between the genuine fun of playing with speeches and scenes and the necessary work towards student facility in expressing what they have discovered. The intention of the student-centred Shakespeare classroom is that all experiences are meaningful and useful, and few, if any, are drudgery.

Our goal in writing this book is to give teachers more ideas and opportunities for the successful teaching of Shakespeare's plays. The materials represent our best thinking through literary scholarship and social science research, and they are intended for flexible use in a student-centred classroom. We offer resources that should build any teacher's confidence in the content, even as some knowledge may have to be subtly hidden so that students can be led to make their own discoveries.

If a student-centred classroom truly allows all kinds of knowledge and ideas into discussion, there will be times when new insights or hard questions will leave us, as instructors, breathless. Welcoming ideas that are not part of the lesson plan can be discombobulating to new teachers and to veterans, particularly if their orientation is to 'tell' Shakespeare. Teachers need to interrogate the impetuses behind, and the consequences of, teacher-centred teaching. What is the goal of telling, interpreting or predigesting Shakespeare for students? Is there some content that *must* be imparted to them? Can students be meaningfully tested on parroted knowledge and interpretations? What relationships can students have to Shakespeare outside the classroom if they are implicitly told 'the answer'?

Many fear that student-centred learning will devolve into chaos, especially if there is no authority. We believe that the teacher's task is not to abdicate control but to organize the classroom, approaching Shakespeare's plays through clearly articulated frames. Teachers who plan to teach Shakespeare's plays in student-centred classrooms encourage advanced learners to recognize that there are many authorities (especially for literary interpretation) and multiple contesting truths. They enable students to listen to their own voices, as well as to recognize that their voices can be in dialogue with many potential authorities. In student-centred classrooms, advanced learners gain the intellectual tools that build their confidence, and they discover that the end of a class or a particular study only marks one stage in an ongoing journey.

As we will emphasize throughout this book, we love Shakespeare's texts, in performance and on the page, and we are determined to share this passion with students. But though we attest to the pleasures of complex texts, what we owe advanced learners are the opportunities, and the appropriate scaffolding for their abilities, to find these joys for themselves.

We have forced ourselves to be mindful of the limitations on good teaching throughout the chapters that follow. Some of these constraints are structural, but others are self-imposed. We have come to call these constraints *The Tyrannies* because teachers feel enormous pressure – both real and internalized – to adhere to them.

Time: No good teacher has enough time, especially when it comes to Shakespeare. How much time does it take to teach *Hamlet*? Teachers must divide a term or the year among works and activities. Once that schedule is set or agreed upon, it is often difficult to alter to follow the interests or pace of the students. Furthermore, average class sessions in the UK and the US range from forty-five minutes to ninety minutes, which fragments attention, focus and expression. When a complete Shakespeare production is viewed live or on a screen, it must occur outside that typical class time band or be experienced in sections.

Space: The number of bodies in a given classroom and how that classroom is physically configured are other structural constraints. There is no definitive research on the optimal class size for an active Shakespeare class.[8] Many teachers dream of fewer students in a larger, more flexible space (e.g. desks that easily move). Almost no teacher has the perfect space; it is a true constraint.

Texts: There is a vast difference in the UK and the US as to what Shakespeare editions are used and how his work is packaged for students. Many teachers do not have control over what edition, and in what format, works are delivered to the students. US textbooks typically contain extensive if wide-ranging notes on language and history. Scholarly editions, like the Arden Shakespeare series, provide glosses and extensive notes on textual variations. There are also editions like *No Fear Shakespeare* that attempt to ease student access through translations of Shakespeare's Elizabethan and Jacobean language. The material constraints of any given school will affect what editions are adopted.

Technology: Innovation outpaces almost any school. We will give advice in the following chapters about digital tools, and this advice will immediately date the book. Some schools have every new gadget and they get updated frequently; other schools have no funds to acquire them. Technology is a material constraint when students ask questions that they do not have the tools to answer (e.g. what did Othello look like in US performances during the Civil War?).

Teacher isolation: Students prosper when teachers have sufficient time to plan together.[9] Many schools do not have the financial resources to structure in the time necessary for collaborative class preparation. Furthermore, many schools lack a culture that encourages teachers to learn from each other or to share ideas and materials.

Student ability: Most teachers cannot control which students are in their classrooms. Our experiences are with 15–20 year olds in an array of publically and privately funded institutions. Some of these students are academically driven, and others are merely enduring their schooling. Some are inclined to drama, some are gifted writers and some perform best in classroom debates. Some are international students and English language learners. As anyone who has taught Shakespeare to 15–20 year olds knows, almost every student struggles with Shakespeare as a text to

---

[8]For an extensive discussion of what is and is not known about optimal class size (not only for teaching Shakespeare), see Darling-Hammond, Ross and Milliken, 'High School Size, Organization, and Content: What Matters for Student Success?'.
[9]For analysis of the consequences of the isolation of US teachers, see Berry, *Teaching 2030: What We Must Do for Our Students and Our Public Schools: Now and in the Future*.

be read. Because we recognize the diverse interests and ability levels of our students as a structural constraint, we offer multiple avenues for students to be successful in the Shakespeare classroom. Many books claim that they can guide teachers to differentiate and meet the needs of every learner; we are not claiming that! Instead, we expect teachers to know their students and to gauge the appropriateness of the activities and materials in this book for their specific classrooms. We are writing for the ambitious teacher who seeks to develop the literacies, talents and global perspectives of all her students. In a student-centred classroom advanced learners are more likely to develop an enthusiasm for grappling with complex texts.

The first step in tackling a tyranny is acknowledging it as such. An individual teacher cannot ignore, wish-away or control institutional constraints, and yet she must find a way to work productively within those limits. Many teaching habits and decisions can result from unconscious *Self-Imposed Tyrannies*. These tyrannies are more insidious: they are not structural or institutional. While it is possible to trace teacher practices back to their likely origins, we have found it more instructive to identify and question *Self-Imposed Tyrannies* related to Shakespeare instruction.[10]

Student diversity: Don't be alarmed, gentle reader, but you may feel uncomfortable at times. We have learned to be comfortable talking about the race, gender, sexuality and physical ability of our students, and we are determined to open dialogues about these topics in our classrooms and yours. While it may look like a diverse classroom is a structural constraint, such perceived limits are self-imposed. Many educators espouse the adage that Shakespeare is for everyone but in practice the rich differences among the students are ignored, thereby rendering those differences unmentionable and irrelevant.

We think it is important to interrogate the purpose and value of being blind to identity differences in the Shakespeare classroom. Who benefits from a race-free, gender-free, sexuality-free and ability-free approach? Who is at an advantage if students are discouraged from sharing observations about identity politics in the plays or in the classroom? Is it sufficient to espouse the value of diversity and not touch upon it in a Shakespeare unit?

We have observed a teacher shutting down a discussion about sexuality because it was clear she feared the class would lose focus, she would lose control and that chaos would ensue. This is a *Self-Imposed Tyranny* that treats discussions of difference as irrelevant to Shakespeare. Where better to talk about complex identity issues than through complex texts? This book demonstrates that there is no better place to talk about complex identity issues than in a classroom that engages Shakespeare's complex texts.

---

[10] For a discussion of how teachers can become caught in unreflective habits, see Britzman, *Practice Makes Practice: A Critical Study of Learning to Teach*.

Coverage/pace: If the structural constraint is time, the self-imposed constraint is coverage. How much Shakespeare counts as covering Shakespeare? In a US secondary school classroom, a Shakespeare teaching unit may focus on plot, character and vocabulary. From Act 1, scene 1 until the closing of Act 5, teachers give all speeches and scenes equal weight because the goal is getting through the play. Along the way students may be asked to identify character names and functions in relation to the plot. They are also often asked to define random vocabulary. In UK schools, the focus for advanced learners is primarily on developing abilities to write examination essays analysing specified plays. In contrast to US schools, instructional designs seem able to include more in-depth study of particular passages, and coursework frequently prepares students to attend to uses of poetic language and literary allusions. As a result classroom practice is typically teacher-centred, with the students concentrating on capturing as much information as possible about the text as delivered and explained by the instructor.

An entirely different coverage model exists in introductory collegiate classrooms, in which it is frequently assumed that more is better: more Shakespeare plays covered in a semester = more knowledge acquisition = more value for one's tuition. What is the end goal? What should the students take away from the unit or course? Even when teachers know that the plots of Shakespeare's plays were not original to him (he frequently lifted from Ovid, Holinshed, Marlowe and others), the coverage model persists. What is the cost to students? Why should Shakespeare matter to these students? Why should these dimensions of a Shakespeare play matter beyond the classroom?

We are not opposed to teaching every word of every play. Our book, however, provides alternatives and asks teachers to re-evaluate their habits and establish new goals. Teachers should restructure their units to meet these goals, and this may mean covering much less of any given Shakespeare text in order to highlight some scenes, explore some characters and analyse competing versions through a clear lens or frame.

Reclaiming close reading

In the US, the electioneering over and corporate co-opting of the Common Core State Standards (and especially the proposed assessments of those standards) has made even the phrase *close reading* contested for many educators. We have heard veteran teachers describe close reading almost entirely in terms of assessment, as if the skill were only applicable to short excerpts under controlled conditions. This is akin to expecting an orchestra to eschew symphonies and only perform the musical passages that are required for auditions. We recognize that the practice of close reading may, for some students, require short passages (and we offer excerpts from the plays as examples for the exercises we suggest). Nonetheless this book reclaims close reading as one of the deepest (and most rewarding) relationships between the text and the reader. We want advanced learners to have the skills to read, enact, hear or witness a Shakespeare play and any other complex text because these skills are necessary in most fields and careers.

Close reading means focused attention on a small amount of text. In practice, this means a text is read over and over again, and for the purposes of this book we mean read silently but also: read aloud, read chorally or enacted; and texts may be listened to, or seen performed. Students should be guided to think about the imagery, language, sounds (including rhyming), repetition and content. They need to become confident in selecting key terms, phrases and images, learning to notice the minutiae. This is hard work, not often an innate skill and it is not overtly valued by our twenty-first-century society. Nonetheless many twenty-first-century learners are practising close reading skills in their informal learning communities. For example, they closely read virtual landscapes and work collaboratively to journey through them successfully. Think about how new players enter and navigate the intricacies of World of Warcraft, SIMS and Grand Theft Auto, and the identities they explore, borrow and appropriate in those virtual worlds.[11] Furthermore, focused attention to detail in complex texts is a central key to power in the 'non' virtual world (e.g. lawyers, doctors, journalists, teachers and entrepreneurs all employ close reading skills).

The next challenge is to develop a student's ability to move from the micro to the macro: from observations of details to a coherent argument about the set of details that leads to an idea of significance. Ultimately the ability to perform close readings distinguishes between those who think they know what a complex text says (or have previously been told what the text says), and those who can independently grapple, wrestle and tease out subtle details that matter.

Students then need to learn how to explain the significance of the evidence they have combined. Highlighting patterns is not the same intellectual work as articulating how and why they matter. Moreover, plot points are not matters of interpretation or argumentation; retelling them should not be mistaken for analytical work. They need to consider why the evidence is included in the play, how the pattern they have identified emphasizes or challenges a central theme or issue in the text and why any

---

[11] Sabatino, 'Improving Writing Literacies through Digital Gaming Literacies: Facebook Gaming in the Composition Classroom'.

literary device is employed. Students need to be taught to ask questions about the evidence they have compiled, determining its significance. These skills must be developed in multiple modes of expression: reading, writing, speaking and listening. It is not enough to expect students to do this in the literary essay only. They need to practise in different modes in order to gain facility with complex texts, which is the purpose of all this work.

As a result of our belief in the primacy of close reading, we expect that every Shakespeare unit will require a teacher to model close reading techniques as one step toward eventually demanding that her advanced learners perform them independently. By *model* it is fair to say *perform*: the teacher should prepare to painstakingly explicate and argue an interpretation of a short passage in order to demonstrate the focus and attention to detail that close reading requires. The teacher must model, as a writing teacher would model drafting and revising, identifying her moves as she considers how a given passage, speech or scene can be read.

We do not recommend that this modelling be wholly extemporaneous! It is in preparing students to take on the work of close reading that we think teachers should put the most concentrated effort. And, at the same time, the teacher should reveal that the thoughtful interpretation/ analysis she offers is one reading among many (in fact, it can be powerful when advanced learners hear close readings that contradict each other). We recognize that such teaching is significantly more demanding than preparing a study guide or quizzing students on plot points. We intend this book as an argument for making this investment in advanced learners and as an aid in the pedagogical content knowledge of teachers.

Authoritarian teaching: Shakespeare's cultural capital functions as a structural constraint. The substantial weight of his works and international cultural legacy can function as a paralytic and a lure. Of course, this is larger than the structural constraints of any one institution, and yet it is a very real factor for any who want or must teach his works. Shakespeare is paralysing for teachers when they try to funnel centuries of scholarship into their lessons. They become dispensers of received Shakespeare, imparting what they believe to be foundational knowledge. While these teachers probably do not view themselves as authoritarian, they may not realize the extent to which their teaching units are offering prescribed and closed interpretations. Likewise, the lure of Shakespeare is potent. Some teachers embrace an opportunity to teach a Shakespeare text because they assume it has a cultural relevance for their students. While they are not wrong, this lure can also lead to a type of authoritarian teaching in which they explain these complex, culturally rich texts to the students who 'need' them.

Even in the excitement to share what a teacher sees or discovers, she can unwittingly undermine collaborative learning.

Our book promotes ways to teach Shakespeare's works as living texts that cannot be boiled down into a congealed interpretation. The unintended consequence of authoritarian teaching is that Shakespeare is dead on the page. A charismatic teacher may make the work 'interesting', but it will not be vital. We champion Shakespeare's multiplicity in all facets – in interpretations, performances and histories – bounded only by the text and its many editions.

Reader response: Many teachers who recognize the pitfalls of authoritarian teaching embrace a reader-response lens.[12] They fear that Shakespeare will be dead on the page if students do not have a personal relationship with the stories, themes and characters. A facile model of reader response inadvertently values relevance over analysis: the personal response is the goal in and of itself.[13] While this may look like the polar opposite of authoritarian teaching, it is actually the flip side of the same coin. In both cases, student analysis of the text – collaborative or individual – is devalued.

Reader-response approaches ask students to imagine themselves in the time or situation of a text because personal relevance is the vehicle for understanding. Why does it matter how students feel about Shakespeare? Obviously it matters in terms of anyone's motivation, but what is the teacher's obligation to stretch her advanced learners' thinking? If relevance is important for knowledge acquisition, what moves diverse student populations toward more sophisticated expressions of their ideas? Can a class debate the meaning and significance of a text if the requested response is merely emotional or personal?

Relevance should be an open question to be discussed, interrogated and debated in the Shakespeare classroom. We agree with Deborah Appleman's claim that reader-response is one of many lenses for approaching complex texts, but we stress that no single lens is adequate in and of itself and none is useful without a guiding purpose. Because we are concerned with advanced learners, we value instructional designs that are explicit both for teachers and students, where the goals are shared and frames intentional.

---

[12] For a thoughtful and extensive discussion of the benefits and challenges of reader-response theory in the teaching of critical analysis to adolescents, see Appleman, *Critical Encounters in High School English: Teaching Literary Theory to Adolescents.*

[13] Clearly such a facile response would not be advocated in Louise M. Rosenblatt's seminal work on reader response: *The Reader, the Text, the Poem: The Transactional Theory of the Literary Work.*

How to use this book

Teaching Shakespeare with Purpose shows teachers how to approach Shakespeare's works as vehicles for collaborative exploration, to develop intentional frames for discovery and to release the texts from over-determined interpretations. In other words, *Teaching Shakespeare with Purpose* presents how to teach Shakespeare's plays to diverse advanced learners as living, breathing and evolving texts. Each chapter concentrates on one Shakespeare play: *Hamlet* (Chapter 2), *Othello* (3), *Romeo and Juliet* (4), *The Merchant of Venice* (5), *Julius Caesar* (6), *A Midsummer Night's Dream* (7) and *Macbeth* (8).

If you are a teacher who does not have time to read this book cover to cover, we recommend reading Chapter 2 to understand our approach for reimagining a Shakespeare unit. Chapter 2 delineates how to get started within a framed pedagogical approach, offering new ways for educators to think about constructing and teaching such a unit. The purpose is to build a student's facility with complex texts, which we view as a fundamental and transferable skill set. Advanced learners value classrooms that incorporate their twenty-first-century learning habits: participation in informal learning communities, explicit exploration of identity, divergent paths to information and innovative performances of knowledge. We discuss how creating a framed approach allows educators to choose specific scenes to examine, relevant historical information to discuss, informed performance clips to analyse and critical approaches to debate.

Chapters 3, 4 and 5 provide twenty-first-century frames for constructing new units that build on common approaches to Shakespeare's texts. For example, Chapter 3 focuses on Shakespeare's language. When we surveyed educators about what worries them most about teaching Shakespeare, they overwhelmingly indicated that it is Shakespeare's language. In this chapter, we present a solution: an approach that does not position the instructor as the authority or translator of Renaissance English; instead we encourage a collective approach to grappling with Shakespeare's language. When educators eschew positioning themselves as the single authority on the text and its meanings, students can explore the difficulties of the 400-year-old English as an informal learning community. And while we endorse the familiar *Oxford English Dictionary* (OED) language exercise – to look up a specific word to identify its meaning and uses in the Renaissance – we also promote performance-based methods of language decoding. The dynamism in language (the way English words change meaning over time) is nothing to be feared; rather, it is a rewarding challenge when approached collectively.

Chapter 4 tackles the common incorporation of performance-based practices in the Shakespeare classroom. The student's body plays a central role in his/her kinaesthetic processes and syntheses, yet the current theories, methodologies and practices of performance-based pedagogy sacrifice discussions of the student's race, gender, ability and sexuality in order to espouse a universalist rhetoric. We provide strategies for focusing tableau, movement exercises and excerpted scripts in order to demonstrate what our diversity brings to interpretation and expression. In addition, we discuss guidelines for intentional, explicit and safe explorations of difference.

Chapter 5 reimagines approaches to history in the Shakespeare classroom. Many educators celebrate the fact that they can bind together history, literature and culture when they teach Shakespeare's plays. This is absolutely the case, but this chapter asks educators to think about which history they highlight and why. Are these plays only about the historical moment in which they were written? We know, for example, that the interpretations and performances of *The Merchant of Venice* have changed significantly since the Holocaust. Isn't the history of the Holocaust as relevant as Shakespeare's own history in the classroom? Because we approach Shakespeare's plays as dynamic organisms whose meanings and performances develop, accrue and metamorphose over time, we invite students to imagine and discover if, when and how different readers and audience members have been affected by the plays. We invite instructors to consider how Shakespeare's plays, while distinct historical events, are never entirely isolated or separate.

Chapters 6 and 7 address outcomes for the reimagined Shakespeare unit. In particular, Chapter 6 explores writing assignments within a purposeful instructional design. This chapter illustrates how students can produce significant analytical writing after extended practical and critical encounters with one or more of the plays. We help instructors craft essay assignments that lead to work that cannot be purchased on *Google*. Students need to be required to synthesize embodied practices, rich classroom discussions and analytical texts in a purposeful Shakespeare classroom. For the most ambitious instructors, we offer powerful options for pushing students to high levels of creation and evaluation in response to a Shakespeare play. We encourage instructors to create writing assignments that recognize that some students thrive as theorists while others approach texts as artists.

In Chapter 7 we urge educators to abandon assessments that focus on surface-level material, including study guides, 'checks for understanding' and plot sequence quizzes. Instead we promote small scale and informal writing assignments. These can allow instructors to hold students accountable for participation, and give students a foundation for more sophisticated arguments. Many instructors complain that performance-based pedagogical approaches are difficult to assess. In this chapter we provide some assessment rubrics that enable both student reflection and performance evaluation.

Teaching Shakespeare with Purpose concludes with a series of applications of our approach to teaching Shakespeare to advanced learners. The applications are divided and organized according to the approaches

Students learning through performance. By kind permission of Braeburn International School Arusha.

we have discussed in each preceding chapter. These applications are not intended to comprise a unit of study; rather, they are meant to illustrate strategies that teachers can adapt as they work to increase their particular students' facility with complex texts.

We close each chapter by advancing multiple strategies for teachers to put the theoretical frame into practice, and we set off these sections under the heading 'Twenty-first-century Teaching and Learning'. Focusing on a single Shakespeare play, we suggest entry points, frames, guiding questions, sample texts, discussion, activity and writing prompts, and interpretive questions for collective debate.

We struggled to find images that are appropriate for teaching advanced learners Shakespeare. In the end, we decided to include images almost entirely from twenty-first-century performances to illustrate interpretive choices. We selected these images based on our belief in the pedagogical utility of juxtaposition. Some images include period costumes, some include single-sex casting, some include non-traditional casting and many are images from global, non-English-speaking productions. While we have prioritized contemporary productions, there are many resources available to teachers who feel they need additional historical images. The Folger Shakespeare Library's Digital Images collection is a fantastic free resource.[14] And as any teacher of our advanced learners knows, for every one image we can find, they will have fifty.

Because Shakespeare's plays are excellent vehicles for many topics – history, socio-cultural norms and mores, vocabulary, rhetoric, literary tropes and terminology, performance history, performance strategies, etc. – it is tempting to teach his plays as literary spinach – texts that are good for everything. This lens-free, grab-bag approach, however, often centres the classroom on the teacher as the expert and renders Shakespeare's plays as fixed, determined and dead. *Teaching Shakespeare with Purpose* demonstrates how to create the appropriate frames for instruction that free educators from total-coverage models and facilitate student investigation.

---

[14] The Folger Shakespeare Library's Digital Images collection is available online for free: http://luna.folger.edu/luna/servlet/FOLGERCM1~6~6.

2

Frames and entry points: Getting to the 'first day' with a Shakespeare text

So, where to start and how to start? Shakespeare's texts can seem challenging and overwhelming with their fascinating plots, beautiful language, interesting characters and thought-provoking themes. When crafting a unit, teachers may also consider the complex history of the Elizabethan and Jacobean world in which Shakespeare created, and the complicated history of his plays in performance over the course of four centuries. When there are so many rich angles, where and how is an educator supposed to begin?

In Chapter 1, we emphasized the ultimate purpose of teaching Shakespeare in the twenty-first-century world: to enable advanced learners to develop an independent facility with complex texts. This book helps teachers to do this by combining the analytical strategies of Shakespeare scholarship with what social scientists know about the habits of learning. Our combined expertise allows us to offer unique approaches to planning and starting Shakespeare instruction.

In this chapter we explore the term *frame* to describe a delimited, intentional and focused approach to the multiplicity of interpretive lenses available. We also discuss strategies for choosing when, where and why to enter the text in class: we call these moments *entry points*. Throughout the chapter the work of *close reading* is prioritized. We suspect that every Shakespeare unit will require a teacher to model, perhaps multiple times, close readings of passages, speeches or scenes. The modelling we imagine is parallel to how writing teachers demonstrate revision choices through a kind of out-loud close reading of their works-in-progress. Nancie Atwell refers to this modelling technique as one that takes 'off the top of my head', as if students could watch the neurons firing in her brain.[1] Teaching Shakespeare requires such a demonstration, so that students can witness

---

[1] Atwell, *In the Middle: New Understandings about Writing, Reading, and Learning*, 331.

how a reader creates an interpretation of a speech or scene by selecting and parsing key words and phrases and then examining and crafting those details into a well-reasoned argument. The teacher should reveal her analytical thinking (meta-cognitive moves) so that the process of analysis is transparent.

While the world is full of books about how to teach Shakespeare (as our bookshelves can attest), our unique contribution is to provide strategies for interrogating, choosing and employing strategic interpretive lenses and effective pedagogical approaches. Our expertise in both literary scholarship and social science research informs our approach to planning and starting the study of a Shakespeare play, with specific examples for beginning a unit on *Hamlet*. What follows below should help teachers (*a*) plan how they will model a close reading; (*b*) determine how they will 'step out' at strategic points to highlight their analytical choices and reasoning; and (*c*) structure the class discussion.

Prior knowledge

Social science research pays attention to prior learning by reminding teachers to start instruction where the students are; good teachers are mindful of what the advanced learners in their classrooms may bring to the study of a Shakespeare play. Teachers consider what expectations the students may have, for instance, for the conventions of playwriting. These educators recognize that students will bring fragmentary or incomplete understandings, including preconceived notions and prejudices. Teachers also recognize that advanced learners may be industrious and uncritical consumers of SparkNotes or Wikipedia.

Especially at the secondary school level, teachers know that they must activate the students' prior knowledge in order to build on it, and they do this because students who have reason to think about what they already know typically find they can make better connections to new knowledge and build significant memory. Introductory activities that access prior knowledge lead students to become engaged rather than passive readers of a complex text.

As a Shakespeare unit begins, the educator should consider what activities or events in their classroom will enable students to express and share what they already know from their lives as well as their formal and informal learning. As Norma Gonzalez and Luis Moll have articulated, students bring funds of knowledge – their own experiences, cultures and histories – to the classroom, and thus to a Shakespeare play.[2] Teachers

---

[2]Gonzalez and Moll, 'Cruzando el Puente: Building Bridges to Funds of Knowledge', 625.

may start with thematic explorations, encouraging students to imagine and describe frayed friendships, inexplicable parents or miserable loves.

Teachers who are concerned about student resistance to Shakespeare's language (see Chapter 3) can find a wealth of resources, such as those the Folger Shakespeare Library Education team calls 'on-ramps', that bring students into a play through active approaches, using excerpts and phrases to bring more comfort with unexpected diction and metaphoric language.

As we wrote in Chapter 1, we believe that students should be given the plot and the characters because a true facility with complex texts requires much more than recalling plot summaries. Theatre-based classroom techniques (see Chapter 4), such as the popular 'Whooosh' activity, created by the Royal Shakespeare Company, are one way that teachers can introduce the bare bones of the plot and allow students to have a starting place for recognizing who is who in the drama.

We can imagine a classroom in which it might be appropriate to start with some aspect of Shakespeare's life and times, particularly if the chosen frame includes Renaissance history and the perspective of the play itself in other histories (see Chapter 5). Some teachers may believe that their students need initial opportunities to become accustomed to terminology or vocabulary, or to be reminded of what they already know about literary devices or even previously studied Shakespeare plays.

Activating prior knowledge has a fundamental purpose: to prepare the class for the close reading of the Shakespeare text itself. Many teachers utilize Madeline Hunter's 'anticipatory sets' to connect the world of the students to the subject at hand.[3] However, we believe an effective Shakespeare unit requires a teacher to model, perhaps multiple times, close readings of passages, speeches or scenes. Such modelling is that much more effective when students recognize what they know (or believe they know) *confirmed and challenged* by the text itself. Advanced learners gain independent facility with complex texts when their teachers: (*a*) demonstrate a close reading while enumerating their analytical moves; (*b*) acknowledge contradictory readings and/or interpretive lenses; and (*c*) facilitate dynamic class discussions of specific passages through specific frames.

---

[3] This terminology is so widely used in US lesson planning pedagogy that it is good to remember with whom it all began: Hunter and Hunter, *Madeline Hunter's Mastery Teaching: Increasing Instructional Effectiveness in Elementary and Secondary Schools.*

Frames

The time we have to teach advanced learners a Shakespeare text is never limitless, but even if it were we believe it is beneficial to plan through specific frames, designing instruction within a topic or a set of topics. A frame provides a focused approach that delimits and organizes the class's movement through the play. Literary scholarship offers any number of topics for the study of *Hamlet*, including political history, mourning, revenge, the purpose of playing/use of performance, blended-family dynamics, gender politics, etc. A teacher must choose and prioritize from such topics in order to create a frame, a focused approach. Furthermore, this delimiting decision organizes her materials, discussions, assignments and assessments toward the purpose: building student facility with complex texts. Later, as they become increasingly independent learners, students will eventually choose their own frames.

We want teachers to choose a frame that allows them to value and prioritize the purpose (facility with complex texts) even as they cope with the constraints of time and resources. Teachers must decide what role recordings, videos and online materials will play in the unit. We are not dogmatic about particular resources, because the frame should dictate if, how and when any are employed.

In a unit on *Hamlet* there are any number of potential frames. What follows are some of our favourites:

Familial relations: A great unit on *Hamlet* might be framed by an interrogation of familial relations. There are several father–son relations depicted in the play: Old Hamlet, the deceased King of Denmark, and Prince Hamlet; Polonius and Laertes; and Old Fortinbras, the deceased King of Norway, and Prince Fortinbras. There are also mother–son relations depicted with Gertrude and Hamlet, and brother–sister relations with Laertes and Ophelia. Just as importantly, there are noticeable absences in certain family structures (e.g. Laertes' and Ophelia's mother).

Remembrance: Death, mourning and one's desire to remember are central to *Hamlet*. The ghost of Hamlet, after all, implores his son to remember him. Likewise, Ophelia gives specific flowers to her brother to spur him to remember. And Hamlet's dying words to Horatio are a request to ensure that his story is remembered.

Revenge: *Hamlet* is a revenge tragedy that centres on Hamlet's desire to avenge his father's death. Yet Hamlet is not the only character who seeks revenge: Laertes and Fortinbras seek revenge against Hamlet himself.

Purpose of playing: *Hamlet* famously contains a play-within-the-play. Yet that is not the only moment in the text that comments on the purpose of playing. In fact, several characters including Hamlet and Polonius seem to have extensive prior experience with theatre (Hamlet as an attentive audience member and Polonius as an actor). Likewise, acting is employed by several characters in their day-to-day lives: Hamlet feigns madness; Polonius directs Ophelia's actions toward Hamlet; and Rosencrantz and Guildenstern pretend not to be spying on Hamlet.

The problem with women: Although the women in the play are innocent of the major crimes committed at Elsinore, Hamlet rails that frailty is unique to women's nature. He casts doubts on his mother's fidelity because she remarries, and he insults Ophelia's chastity. Hamlet seems to think there is something inherently wrong with women.

A frame, then, focuses on a specific delimited topic, or set of topics, to organize the class's way through the text, and guiding questions help to prioritize, organize and focus attention to the frame. The best guiding questions are thorny, provocative and large, and they are not obvious or fact based (e.g. the questions 'How does Polonius die?' and 'Why does Laertes want revenge?' are not effective guiding questions because they are plot based). In the chapters that follow we provide sample guiding questions that require advanced learners to wade through and interrogate portions of the text; answers to the questions should necessitate more than one quotation. The guiding questions that we provide are intended to spur close reading and text-based discussion in order to explore a chosen frame as deeply as appropriate. Ideally in a student-centred classroom, advanced learners will create and pursue their own guiding questions (see Chapter 6 for the ways writing assignments support this).

In a unit on *Hamlet* the guiding questions will lead students into the text. If we build on the frames listed above, some potential guiding questions are:

Frame: Familial relations
Guiding question:
What is the difference between brothers and fathers; between brothers and lovers?

Frame: Remembrance
Guiding question:
Why do people use physical markers or places to remember the dead? What does this say about death, mourning and memory?

Frame: Revenge
Guiding question:
Why do so many of the sons in *Hamlet* act as if revenge is the only recourse they have to prove their love and loyalty to their fathers?

Frame: Purpose of playing
Guiding question:
    Hamlet seems to be very familiar with theatre, but he also distrusts performance. How does he navigate this tension?

Frame: The problem with women
Guiding question:
    In Hamlet's mind, what is wrong with women, and how can they be 'fixed'?

The guiding questions above are informed by various interpretive lenses. It may surprise some educators to realize that frames are never free from interpretive lenses. For example, one teacher may have fallen in love with Mel Gibson's performance in the 1990 film version of *Hamlet*. Because of that love, she may want to focus on the role of mothers as a frame. While that is a great topic, to construct an effective Shakespeare unit the teacher needs to be conscious of the fact that this frame is informed by a Freudian interpretive lens that should be questioned collectively. The teacher's guiding questions should lead advanced learners to interrogate the Freudian interpretive lens and how it gets enacted. To build independent facility with a complex text the teacher should also highlight the meta-cognitive moves she is making as she uses the frame. The teacher might say, 'I am asking questions about the play's representation of motherhood because, in a Freudian interpretive lens, the mother–son relationship is prioritized above all others as fundamental in human development.' In this way the teacher demonstrates the reasoning behind her choices for highlighting certain aspects of the text (i.e. meta-cognitive statements).

    In moving students through a Shakespeare text, a teacher should intentionally employ multiple interpretive lenses. Depending on the level of the learner, it may be appropriate to name these lenses. For example, in the introductory university classroom, labels like 'Freudian', 'New Historicist' or 'Marxist' may be beneficial from the beginning of their use in the classroom; however, a secondary classroom may need more exposure to multiple and diverse critical perspectives without the distraction of labels. In both cases, the important thing is that the teacher explicitly signals that no single interpretive lens is ever sufficient.[4]

    Students who become wedded to a single interpretive lens may be especially helped by an instructional design that includes multiple editions. By editions we mean both the historical editions printed in the Renaissance and the modern edited editions included in textbooks and free-standing volumes. Students are frequently stunned to learn that Shakespeare's texts are not stable, that there were multiple conflicting versions printed during and after

---

[4]Appleman, *Critical Encounters in High School English: Teaching Literary Theory to Adolescents*, 9.

Shakespeare's lifetime. Modern editions frequently erase these instabilities through editorial practice: the revelation of this fact demonstrates that editing is interpretation.[5] Classrooms in the UK and other places that use the Arden Shakespeare editions have access to copious notes on conflicting editions (fifty or more pages in the introduction of *Hamlet* are devoted to the play's textual variants). When the instructional design includes attention to textual editions, the teacher reinforces the priority of analysis over implied authority.

Editions used in UK and US classrooms

As teachers frame their approach to a Shakespeare play they determine what will count as a text, and what proportion of that text is appropriate for their students. In general we think a full play is preferable to excerpts, especially when the excerpts are presented out of context, but we have seen teachers make meaningful pairings of scenes from complementary Shakespeare plays in order to explore a particular frame.

Secondary students in the UK typically have a copy of a given play to read from a class set, and it is not unusual for various students to be consulting Cambridge, Globe or other 'student' editions within the same classroom. In the US, students are more likely to have a Shakespeare play embedded in a standard textbook or anthology. Having students pay attention to differing editions of plays is an important way to communicate the instability and dynamism of the texts.

Teachers in both countries utilize 'modern translation' editions, and we recognize that English language learners and other students can benefit from materials that supplement the text, including judiciously utilized graphic novels and pared-down scripts. Teachers may also distribute copies in order to encourage students to annotate the text to various purposes; such marking and highlighting is a significant activity in any close reading. Students who use copies of scenes to create scripts for themselves can come to understand the challenge of editing for performance (see Chapter 6 for editing as part of a written assignment).

Even in the situation in which teachers are not choosing the particular edition of a Shakespeare play, or cannot afford individual student copies for marking, the frame should help them determine the extent to which they will reference the marginalia and notes that a publisher may offer. The useful boundaries of the chosen frame can allow teachers and students to utilize the notes that scaffold meaning and ignore materials that are a distraction or not relevant to the particular focus.

---

[5]The first three chapters in Stephen Orgel's book, *The Authentic Shakespeare*, are especially good on modern editing practices.

Entry points

By *entry point* we mean the first portion of text the teacher introduces and unpacks through modelled close reading and facilitated discussion. Having observed many typical Shakespeare units in secondary and university settings, we know the habit of beginning at the beginning. Sometimes this decision works well if the unit is framed around a central question from the play, such as in *Hamlet*, 'Who's there?' (1.1.1). Guiding questions indicate the direction we move through the text. While the frame is the larger topic – or set of topics – the guiding questions provide substantive ways to read closely and create arguments. Beginning in Act 1, scene 1, enables the class to focus on why it is difficult to determine and distinguish individuals (characters share names, Polonius is confused for Claudius and the Ghost is what?), and the beginning of the play is an effective place to start.

It is not necessary to start at the beginning of the play, though, because the frame should guide the entry point. For example, another teacher might choose to start the unit with the Ghost demanding, 'Remember me' (1.5.91). By not starting at the beginning, the teacher can delimit the text to focus on the differences between revenge and remembrance. A third teacher might begin with Laertes' warning to Ophelia that Hamlet's 'will is not his own, / For he himself is subject to his birth' (1.3.17–18), intentionally framing the unit on characters' observations of each other. In each case, the teacher is organizing the unit by prioritizing a topic over linear coverage. Some teachers will find it easier to choose a frame before choosing a corresponding entry point; others will find it easier to choose the text first. The sequence of choosing the frame and entry point is less important than the teacher's readiness to model a close reading. An *entry point* is the best way to insert a specific and selected text into the students' general knowledge of a Shakespeare play and the connections they may have already made to the selected frame. The entry points we offer are rich texts for the exploration of guiding questions.

Sample Entry Point 1
Frame: Familial relations
Guiding question:
What is the difference between brothers and fathers; between brothers and lovers?
Entry Point: *Hamlet* 1.3.15–50

LAERTES: Perhaps he loves you now,
And now no soil nor cautel doth besmirch
The virtue of his will; but you must **fear**,
His greatness weighed, his will is not his own.
He may not, as **unvalued persons** do,
Carve for himself, for on his choice depends
The safety and health of this whole state,
And therefore must his **choice be circumscribed**
Unto the voice and yielding of that body
Whereof he is the **head**. Then if he says he loves you
It fits your wisdom so far to believe it
As he in his particular act and place
May give his saying deed, which is no further
Than the main voice of Denmark goes withal.
Then weigh what loss you list his songs
Or lose your heart, or your chaste treasure open
To his unmastered importunity.
Fear it, Ophelia, **fear** it, my dear sister,
And keep you in the rear of your affection
Out of the shot and **danger of desire**.
The chariest maid is prodigal enough
If she unmask her beauty to the moon.
Virtue itself scapes not **calumnious** strokes.
The **canker** galls the infants of the spring
Too oft before their buttons be disclosed,
And in the morn and liquid dew of youth
Contagious blastments are most imminent.
Be **wary** then: best safety lies in **fear**,
Youth to itself rebels, though none else near.
OPHELIA: I shall the effect of this good lesson keep
As watchman to my heart. But, good my brother,
Do not as some ungracious pastors do
Show me the steep and thorny way to heaven
Whiles, a puffed and reckless libertine,
Himself the **primrose path of dalliance** treads
And recks not his own rede.

Discussion leading questions:

These remarks are advice from a brother, acting like a father, to a sister, and they represent a brother's take on the relations between lovers. Keeping these facts in mind, the class could discuss the following questions, which are designed to foster their careful attention to the details of the passage (i.e. close reading).

- What is an 'unvalued person' and what can such a person do that Hamlet cannot? Why?
- Why must Hamlet's 'choice be circumscribed' if he is the 'head' of the state? What does this say about Laertes' take on Hamlet's free will?
- Notice how often Laertes uses the verb 'fear'. What should Ophelia fear? Why?
- Why does Laertes discuss his sister's desire in terms of 'danger'? And what do you make of his use of the words 'calumnious', 'canker' and 'contagious'?
- How does Ophelia respond to her brother's advice? What exactly is a 'primrose path of dalliance'?

Sample Entry Point 2
Frame: Remembrance
Guiding question:
  Why do people use physical markers or places to remember the dead? What does this say about death, mourning and memory?
Entry Point: *Hamlet* 1.5.91–112

> GHOST   Adieu, adieu, adieu, remember me.   [*Exit.*]
> HAMLET: O all you host of heaven, O earth – what else? –
>   And shall I couple hell? O fie! Hold, hold, my heart,
>   And you, my sinews, grow not instant old
>   But bear me swiftly up. **Remember thee?**
>   Ay, thou poor ghost, whiles memory holds a seat
>   In this distracted globe. **Remember thee?**
>   Yea, from the **table of my memory**
>   I'll wipe away all trivial fond records,
>   All saws of books, all forms, all pressures past
>   That youth and observation copied there
>   And thy commandment all alone shall live
>   Within the **book and volume of my brain**
>   Unmixed with baser matter. Yes, by heaven,
>   O most pernicious woman,
>   O villain, villain, smiling damned villain,
>   **My tables! Meet it is I set it down**
>   That one may smile and smile and be a villain –
>   At least I am sure it may be so in Denmark.
>   So, uncle, there you are. **Now to my word.**
>   It is '**Adieu, adieu, remember me.**'
>   **I have sworn't.**

Discussion leading questions:
  While the ghost of Hamlet has appeared to others earlier in the play, this represents the first time he has spoken and only Hamlet hears his words. Keeping these facts in mind, the class could discuss the following questions, which are designed to foster their careful attention to the details of the passage (i.e. close reading).

- What words or phrases are repeated and why?
- What is the 'table of my memory'? What exactly will Hamlet write on the tables? Are Hamlet's 'tables' literal or metaphorical? And what is the difference between the two for Hamlet?
- How will anyone know if Hamlet is remembering?
- How is repetition related to memory?

Sample Entry Point 3
Frame: Revenge
Guiding question:
Why do so many of the sons in *Hamlet* act as if revenge is the only recourse they have to prove their love and loyalty to their fathers?
Entry Point: *Hamlet* 4.5.116–47

LAERTES:	Give me my father.
QUEEN:	Calmly, good Laertes.
LAERTES:	That drop of blood that's calm proclaims me **bastard**,
	Cries '**Cuckold!**' to my father, brands the **harlot**
	Even here between the chaste **unsmirched** brow
	Of my true mother.
KING:	What is the cause, Laertes,
	That thy rebellion looks so giant-like?
	Let him go, Gertrude, do not fear our person.
	There's such divinity doth hedge a king
	That treason can but peep to what it would,
	Acts little of his will. Tell me, Laertes,
	Why thou art thus incensed. Let him go, Gertrude.
	Speak, man.
LAERTES:	Where is my father?
KING:	Dead.
QUEEN:	But not by him.
KING:	Let him demand his fill.
LAERTES:	How came he dead? I'll not be **juggled** with.
	To hell allegiance, vows to the blackest devil,
	Conscience and grace to the profoundest pit.
	I dare damnation. To this point I stand –
	That both the worlds I give to negligence.
	Let come what comes, only I'll be revenged
	Most thoroughly for my father.
KING:	Who shall stay you?
LAERTES:	My will, not all the world's.
	And for my means I'll husband them so well
	They shall go far with little.
KING:	Good Laertes,
	If you desire to know the certainty
	Of your dear father, is't writ in your revenge
	That swoopstake **you will draw both friend and foe,**
	Winner and loser?

LAERTES:	None but his enemies.
KING	Will you know them, then?
LAERTES:	To his good friends thus wide I'll ope my arms
	And like the kind life-rendering pelican
	Repast them with my blood.
KING:	Why, now you speak
	Like a good child and a true gentleman.

Discussion leading questions:

Hamlet is not the only character who seeks revenge. In fact, Laertes seeks revenge against Hamlet himself. Keeping these facts in mind, the class could discuss the following questions, which are designed to foster their careful attention to the details of the passage (i.e. close reading).

- Why does Laertes have no intention of being calm? What would a calm demeanour signify to him?

- Why does Laertes equate revenge with damnation? And why is he still willing to risk damnation for revenge?

- How does the King test Laertes' notion of what a good revenge entails? And why/how is he able to call Laertes a 'good child' in the end?

Sample Entry Point 4
Frame: Purpose of playing
Guiding question:
Hamlet seems to be very familiar with theatre, but he also distrusts performance. How does he navigate this tension?
Entry Point: *Hamlet* 1.2.68–86

> QUEEN: Good Hamlet, cast thy **nighted colour** off
> And let thine eye look like a friend on Denmark.
> Do not for ever with thy **vailed lids**
> Seek for thy noble father in the **dust.**
> Thou knowst 'tis common all that lives must die,
> Passing through nature to eternity.
> HAMLET: Ay, madam, it is common.
> QUEEN: If it be
> Why **seems** it so particular with thee?
> HAMLET: 'Seems', madam – nay it is, I know not 'seems'.
> 'Tis not alone my **inky cloak,** cold mother,
> Nor **customary suits of solemn black,**
> Nor **windy suspiration of forced breath,**
> No, nor the **fruitful river in the eye,**
> Nor the **dejected haviour of the visage,**
> Together with all forms, moods, shapes of grief,
> That can denote me truly. These indeed 'seem',
> For they are actions that a man might play,
> But I have that within which passes show,
> These but the trappings and the suits of woe.

Discussion leading questions:
Queen Gertrude urges her son to move beyond grief, but Hamlet seizes on her words to talk instead about the performance of grief. Keeping these facts in mind, the class could discuss the following questions, which are designed to foster their careful attention to the details of the passage (i.e. close reading).

- What does Gertrude mean when she tells Hamlet to 'cast thy nighted colour off'? How should a friend of Denmark look according to the queen?
- Why does Hamlet repeat the word 'common'? What is significant about that word?
- Why does Hamlet repeat the word 'seems'? What is significant about that word?
- Make a list of the physical manifestations of grief that Hamlet enumerates. Why does Hamlet focus on these physical manifestations? What does this say about Hamlet's notion of acting in general?

Sample Entry Point 5
Frame: The problem with women
Guiding question:
In Hamlet's mind, what is wrong with women, and how can they be 'fixed'?
Entry Point: *Hamlet* 1.2.129–59

HAMLET: O that this too too sallied flesh would melt,
Thaw and resolve itself into a dew,
Or that the Everlasting had not fixed
His canon 'gainst self-slaughter. O God, God,
How **weary, stale, flat and unprofitable**
Seem to me all the uses of the world!
Fie on't, ah, fie, 'tis an unweeded garden
That grows to seed, things **rank and gross in nature**
Possess it merely. That it should come to this:
But **two months** dead – nay not so much, not two –
So excellent a king, that was to this
Hyperion to a satyr, **so loving to my mother**
That he might not beteem the winds of heaven
Visit her face too roughly. Heaven and earth,
Must I remember? Why, **she would hang on him**
As if increase of appetite had grown
By what it fed on. And yet **within a month**
(Let me not think on't – **Frailty, thy name is Woman**),
A little month, or e'er those shoes were old
With which she followed my poor father's body,
Like Niobe, all tears. Why, she –
O God, **a beast that wants discourse of reason**
Would have mourned longer – married with my uncle,
My father's brother (but no more like my father
That I to Hercules). **Within a month,**
Ere yet the salt of most unrighteous tears
Had left the flushing in her galled eyes,
She married. **O most wicked speed!** To post
With such dexterity to **incestuous sheets,**
It is not, nor it cannot come to good;
But break, my heart, for **I must hold my tongue.**

Discussion leading questions:
This famous soliloquy begins with Hamlet pondering his own suicide, but then Hamlet makes an unexpected rhetorical turn from mourning to misogyny. Keeping these facts in mind, the class could discuss the following questions, which are designed to foster their careful attention to the details of the passage (i.e. close reading).

- Why does the world seem 'weary, stale, flat and unprofitable' to Hamlet? And what could make the world seem useful to him now?

- Track how Hamlet clocks the months since his father's death? How long has it been? Why does the time shorten during the course of this soliloquy?

- How does Hamlet describe his mother's relationship with his deceased father? What is the evidence he has of his mother failing his father? Is the failure unique to her or inherent in all women according to Hamlet?

- What makes the sheets on his mother's bed 'incestuous'? And why does Hamlet feel he must hold his tongue about it?

Diane Venora as Gertrude and Ethan Hawke as Hamlet in Michael Almereyda's 2000 film Hamlet.

Julie Christie as Gertrude and Kenneth Branagh as Hamlet in Kenneth Branagh's 1996 film Hamlet.

Modelled close reading

As we indicate at the beginning of the chapter, every Shakespeare unit will require a teacher to model close reading techniques before her advanced learners can perform them independently. Moreover, this type of modelling is most effective when the teacher's meta-cognitive moves are made explicit to the students. It is also effective when teachers reveal that their thoughtful interpretations/analyses are simply one reading among many. In fact, it is often very powerful when advanced learners have close readings modelled for them that contradict each other. For instance, there are radically different interpretations of Hamlet's command to Ophelia to, 'Get thee to a nunnery' (3.1.120). While some read this line as a request to protect Ophelia's chastity among a group of celibate nuns, others read this line as an order for Ophelia to become a sex worker (brothels in the early modern period were euphemistically called nunneries). Teachers who model close reading need to remind students that while not everyone will see/interpret/ perform the text in the same way, not all perspectives are equally well argued and are therefore not equally valuable. Simply because there is ambiguity in the text does not mean that all readings are compelling (e.g. it would not be compelling to argue that 'Get thee to a nunnery' means that Hamlet views Ophelia as an illegitimate child).

Advanced learners gain independent facility with complex texts when their teachers: (*a*) demonstrate a close reading while enumerating their analytical moves; (*b*) acknowledge contradictory readings and/or interpretive lenses; and (*c*) facilitate dynamic class discussions of specific passages through specific frames.

Below is an example of a close reading of Ophelia's burial scene in the final act of Hamlet read through the lens of *familial relations*.

Frame: Familial relations
Guiding question:
What is the difference between brothers and fathers; between brothers and lovers?
Entry Point: *Hamlet* 5.1.235–73

LAERTES: O, treble woe
            Fall ten times double on that cursed head
            Whose wicked deed thy most ingenious sense
            Deprived thee of. Hold off the earth a while,
            Till I have caught her once more in mine arms.
                  [*Leaps in the grave.*]
            Now pile your dust upon the quick and dead
            Till of this flat a mountain you have made
            T'o'ertop old Pelion or the skyish head

	Of blue Olympus.
HAMLET:	[*Comes forward.*] What is he whose grief
	Bears such an emphasis, whose phrase of sorrow
	Conjures the wandering stars and makes them stand
	Like wonder-wounded hearers? This is I,
	Hamlet the Dane.
LAERTES:	[*Leaps out and grapples with him.*]
	The devil take thy soul!
HAMLET:	Thou pray'st not well.
	I prithee take thy fingers from my throat,
	For, though I am not splenative rash,
	Yet have I in me something dangerous
	Which let thy wisdom fear. Hold off thy hand.
KING:	Pluck them asunder.
QUEEN:	Hamlet! Hamlet!
LORDS:	Gentlemen!
HORATIO:	Good my lord, be quiet.
HAMLET:	Why, I will fight with him upon this theme
	Until my eyelids will no longer wag.
QUEEN:	On my son, what theme?
HAMLET:	I loved Ophelia – forty thousand brothers
	Could not with all their quantity of love
	Make up my sum. What wilt thou do for her?
KING:	O, he is mad, Laertes.
QUEEN:	For love of God, forbear him.
HAMLET:	'Swounds, show me what thou'lt do.
	Woul't weep, woul't fight, woul't fast, woul't tear thyself,
	Woul't drink up easel, eat a crocodile?
	I'll do't. Dost come here to whine,
	To outface me with leaping in her grave?
	Be buried quick with her, and so will I.
	And if thou prate of mountains let them throw
	Millions of acres on us till our ground,
	Singeing his pate against the burning zone,
	Make Ossa like a wart. Nay, an thou'lt mouth,
	I'll rant as well as thou.

1 Read the passage aloud (or have it read), perhaps more than once.

2 The frame of *familial relations* establishes the questions to be asked of this passage. Advanced learners often appreciate a teacher who demonstrates how focus on the particularity of the speech/dialogue/bit of text can actually help limit their obligation to explain and explain and explain. Thus, the frame helps to delimit the immensity of the topics and ideas that *Hamlet* could be about.

3 The modelling reader asks herself: what is the difference between brothers and lovers? It may be important to remind advanced learners that this is the first time Laertes and Hamlet speak to each other in the course of the play (i.e. although they appear together in 1.3, they do not address each other directly until 5.1). The reader asks: how should brothers and lovers mourn differently? The reader wonders: how is grief and mourning enacted in this scene (i.e. exactly what actions take place)? And: why does mourning necessitate any action whatsoever?

4 The modelling reader asks: why does Laertes begin by literally enumerating his grief for Ophelia ('treble', 'ten' and 'double')? What does it mean to quantify grief, and why does Hamlet take up this rhetoric ('forty thousand brothers')? Why does Laertes emphasize the earthy quality of the grave ('earth', 'dust' and 'mountain')? And why does Laertes leap into the grave? What does the physicality of this mourning signify?

5 Then a teacher can direct her advanced learners to Hamlet's entrance: when Hamlet first speaks in this scene, he asks 'whose grief' is so loud that it makes the stars stand still. And then he declares, 'This is I, / Hamlet the Dane'. Is Hamlet saying that the loud griever is Laertes or himself? It might be instructive to demonstrate how the textual ambiguity could be performed differently (e.g. Hamlet could enter speaking very quietly and mutedly, or he could enter wailing loudly and ranting his lines vociferously).

6 Students need to interrogate to what extent Hamlet and Laertes equate physical suffering with proof of emotional suffering. Why do they fight in this scene? It will be instructive to point the advanced learners to Hamlet's declaration that he 'will fight with [Laertes] upon this theme'. Yet the Queen has to ask 'what theme', before Hamlet says that he loved Ophelia more than 'forty thousand brothers'. Why the comparison?

7 It is important for the teacher (as modelling reader) to show her advanced learners that Hamlet sets up a bizarre 'grief-off', asking Laertes what he will do (including drinking rotten water, 'easel', and eating strange meat, 'crocodile'). Why does Hamlet imagine that Laertes' grief will 'outface' his own? Why does he treat grief as a competition?

8 Then it will be important to remind the advanced learners that there are other characters present in this scene (Queen, King, Priest and Horatio). How do the students understand and imagine the observers' reactions? Is there evidence that either Laertes or Hamlet is conscious of the observers?

9 In the end, students need to think through the ways both Laertes

and Hamlet conceive grieving in performative terms (actions like wailing, jumping, crying and tearing out hair). The question for the close reader to puzzle out is: why can the brother and lover not tolerate the other's performance?

Escaping frames

Frames intentionally delimit discussion and argument so that the focus on the text is tight. Frames not only help to get the discussion started but also help to organize the class's movement through the text (a variety of rich pedagogical suggestions appear in the following chapters). Moreover, frames help to combat indiscriminate speculation and random acts of interpretation. And yet the teacher's selection of the frame should only constrict the movement through the text to the extent that she identifies it as one interpretive lens among many. For advanced learners to have an independent facility with complex texts they should make incremental progress toward articulating, reading and arguing through frames of their own creation. In other words, it is our hope that advanced learners will want to escape from the teacher's selected frames to interrogate frames of their own creation.

For example, an advanced learner who has gained a facility with complex texts might use the modelled close reading described above (Hamlet and Laertes at Ophelia's grave) to consider Horatio's role in the play. She may want to frame her reading of Horatio through Friendship, Survival or the Performance of Perpetual Grief, asking why he survives at the end of the play, why he pledges to tell Hamlet's story in perpetuity and even if that performance of grief would be seen as a competitive one with Hamlet's. Yes, gentle reader, this would be the dream student, one who clearly has an independent facility with complex texts. But that is our ultimate goal: to enable all our advanced learners to read, query and analyse Shakespeare's texts independently and authoritatively.

3

'Ancient English': Shakespeare's language

When we surveyed American secondary teachers about what worries them most about teaching Shakespeare, they overwhelmingly indicated that it is Shakespeare's language. We asked teachers to list the 'Challenges Involved in Teaching Shakespeare', and some representative comments include: 'All the old timey language'; 'How can I get my students to see beyond the wordy, flowery, antiquated language?'; 'The language is "hard to understand"'; 'Language confusion'; and 'Clarifying the language'. In the UK, A-level teachers expressed concerns about their students' fears of Shakespeare's language: '[students] also struggle with a mental block around the language – expecting not to understand anything' and describe 'students' fears of the language'.[1] We are sympathetic to the feeling that Shakespeare's language is challenging. After all, he wrote in a language that is now 400+ years removed from our own.

When teachers describe a desire to 'get through' or 'get past' the language of Shakespeare with their students, it is as if the ultimate goal is some ephemeral 'Shakespeare' divorced from his language. Yet this sets the teacher up to be the expert, the explainer, the glosser and the motivator. And the students are justified in chanting the 'chorus of "I can't"' because they are not required to do or own any Shakespeare. Our goal is to promote student-centred classrooms in which students are responsible for collaborative meaning making.

Students understand that Shakespeare is difficult, but they also understand the cultural capital the study of his plays provides. In past eras, one's ability to use Othello's name as a stand-in for a jealous man would be enough to open some doors. But cultural capital is not enough in the twenty-first century: teachers cannot operate on the assumption that exposing students to 'Shakespeare' is enough to guarantee university and employment readiness. Our focus on Shakespeare pedagogy stems from the fact that his texts are some of the most complex in the English language.

---

[1]Barlow, 'Vox Pop: How to Teach Shakespeare at A Level', 15.

Where better than to learn facility with complex texts than with the mother lode of complexity? In this chapter we use *Othello* to illustrate techniques for collaborative learning.

If a facility with complex texts is required for success in the twenty-first century, an aspect that makes Shakespeare's texts particularly complex is the dynamism of the language. Shakespeare's language is dynamic – it is full of allusions, metaphors and double entendre. For example, Desdemona employs an aural pun when she implores Iago to help her against the accusation of infidelity:

> I cannot say whore:
> It does abhor me now I speak the word;
> To do the act that might the addition earn
> Not the world's mass of vanity could make me.
>   (4.2.163–6)

While Desdemona does not seem to intend the aural pun (abhor and whore), theatre audiences are frequently startled by the homonym because they have never heard those words as being related. The aural pun allows the audience to see something in Desdemona that she does not recognize in herself: she can in fact say 'whore' and does so twice all the while denying her ability to do so.

Shakespeare's language is also dynamic because meaning changes over time. The text is not dead on the page with the meaning solidified by glosses and notes. Shakespeare is alive when new readers, actors and audiences bring new meanings and contexts to old words. Teachers should not fear when their students bring modern contexts to Shakespeare's language. While it may seem that these new contexts will distort 'Shakespeare's meaning', meaning is only achieved through a relationship between the reader and the text.

For example, when Emilia calls Othello a 'blacker devil' (5.2.129), historically the phrase referenced the early modern conception of devils as black in colour (but not necessarily in race).[2] And yet many students will read this phrase in light of modern constructions of race. Both of these readings are right, especially when advanced learners recognize the differences between them. Students do not have to treat the intervening 400 years between the writing of *Othello* and their reading of it as irrelevant. When students are made aware of the differences, they gain insights into the power of language and their own role in meaning making.

It is true that Shakespeare's language can be a challenge in the twenty-first-century classroom, and in this chapter we offer strategies to make

---

[2]For an excellent analysis of early modern constructions of race, see Barthelemy, *Black Face, Maligned Race: The Representation of Blacks in English Drama from Shakespeare to Southerne.*

the challenge manageable and to help teachers escape the role of expert explainer. Focusing on Shakespeare's language, we propose an alternative to teacher-centred classrooms. In student-centred classrooms meaning is collaboratively made, and this can include the use of performance-based classroom techniques to decode Shakespeare's language. We do not think that Shakespeare's texts need to be tamed by translation or dumbed-down versions. Rather, we demonstrate how working through Shakespeare's language collaboratively is both rewarding and productive. We believe that advanced learners are capable of meeting the challenge of Shakespeare's language, but not if the instructional design is avoidant, reductive or authoritarian.

Anxiety and instructional design

It is clear that teachers worry that they must provide a real-time gloss as they move students through the text: one that translates not only 'antiquated language' but also the uses and meanings of literary devices. As a result, teachers fear that they will look like idiots in class if they cannot provide the 'proper' answer. It is also clear that teachers worry that students will 'tune out' for various reasons, including student assumptions that Shakespeare's language is too hard, irrelevant and unnecessary.

These fears often result in an instructional design that is inadvertently avoidant, reductive and authoritarian – in other words teacher-focused classrooms. An instructional design that is avoidant allows students to focus on anything other than the language: historical context, building replicas of The Globe, Shakespeare's biography, etc.[3] It is not that any of these activities are wrong if they are employed to support a clear frame (a guiding topic or set of guiding topics), but when they are used as a 'fun' alternative to the 'work' of close reading they do not lead to a facility with complex texts. An avoidant instructional design operates on the principle that students will not enjoy puzzling out the challenges of Shakespeare's language.

A reductive instructional design operates on the principle that subtle nuances or perplexing ambiguities in the text need to be simplified for students. As a result Shakespeare's language is often predigested for the students. The worst version of a reductive instructional design offers only *No Fear Shakespeare* or other modern translations as the 'Shakespeare' text to be studied. In this design the language is lost, and Shakespeare's text is reduced to plot summaries in 'plain English'.[4] Reductive instructional

---

[3]The 'suburbs' are explained in Peggy O'Brien's introduction to volume 1 of *Shakespeare Set Free: Teaching A Midsummer Night's Dream, Romeo and Juliet, and Macbeth*, xiv.
[4]The *No Fear Shakespeare* series advertises itself as providing 'Plain English' translations of the plays.

design often substitutes quasi fact-based knowledge for analysis. Characters are reduced to single traits or inaccurate labels (Moor = North African[5]). We have already said that we believe students can be given plot summaries and character lists (see Chapter 1) because that knowledge should be a given in order to foster close reading (see Chapter 2).

An inadvertently authoritarian instructional design operates on the principle that Shakespeare needs to be explained. This design places enormous weight on a teacher's shoulders (and almost none on the students'). In terms of teaching Shakespeare's language, an authoritarian design requires the teacher to tell, students to listen and regurgitation stands in for assessment. In telling, the teacher labels the literary devices, explains their significance and hopes the students will be able to identify further examples, such as doing a scavenger hunt for the words *like* and *as*. In another variation on telling, the teacher selects key scenes or speeches and provides a short-hand interpretation for the students (e.g. 3.3 in *Othello* is the scene in which Iago discovers and exposes Othello's fatal flaw). Once again this is authoritarian because the students are not encouraged or allowed to make discoveries about the text; students are made to be passive recipients of Shakespeare's meaning.

The pleasure of puzzling

Advanced learners in the twenty-first century need facility with complex texts. A facility with complex texts does not have to be achieved through pain, but it does require work. In his recent book *A Muse and A Maze*, Peter Turchi describes the craft of writing and the work of reading in terms of the rewards of the effort, or the pleasures of puzzling. 'While we may say that we read to be entertained or enlightened, often we find that the books we return to, the books we find most valuable, are the books that disturb or elude us, defy us in some way, even as they appeal to us.'[6] Teaching complex texts, especially Shakespeare's plays, enables teachers and students to explore the pleasures of grappling with complex ideas and language.

Othello's continued popularity stems in part from its difficulty. Untangling the complex language in the play often enables advanced learners to recognize the complexity of the play's ideas. Framing a unit around the topic of *obedience* a teacher can provide the end of Act 3, scene 3 of *Othello* as the entry point.

---

[5] This is the gloss for Moor in Crowther, *No Fear Shakespeare: Othello*, 4.
[6] Turchi, *A Muse and a Maze: Writing as Puzzle, Mystery, and Magic*, 200.

Witness that here Iago doth give up
The execution of his **wit, hands, heart,**
To wronged Othello's service. Let him **command**
And to **obey** shall be in me remorse
What bloody **business** ever.

(3.3.468–72)

The guiding question might focus students on the differences between obeying a husband and obeying a general. What does it mean to ask to be commanded? To enable the students to answer these guiding questions, the teacher can ask her advanced learners about specific word usage: whom does Iago imagine is witnessing this act? What does it mean to give one's 'wit, hands, [and] heart'? Who will 'command', who will 'obey' and why? And why does it end with 'business'? Does 'business' fit with 'Witness', 'give', 'command' and 'obey'? The temptation is to tell students that Iago is appropriating the language of a marriage rite in order to place his relationship with Othello over that of Desdemona's. Why should the teacher do this work for the students? Advanced learners are entirely capable of recognizing the familiar gesture of giving one's hand and heart as a speech act in marriage.[7] In fact, students frequently experience great pleasure in recognizing their competence with complex texts.

OED exercise: A tool for student ownership

One way to encourage students to experience the pleasure of grappling with linguistic complexity is to introduce them to the *Oxford English Dictionary* (OED). The OED claims to be 'the definitive record of the English language', but it does so by not only giving etymological derivations but also by showing the changing uses and meanings of English words over history. Advanced learners typically consult dictionaries for single meanings of words, and most will never have used the OED before. Introducing students to the OED and creating an exercise that allows them to explore the changing uses and meanings of a specific word can be an enlightening and empowering experience. While there are still some printed editions of the dictionary in school libraries, the OED is now available online for free at www.oed.com; there is also an OED app.

Within the frame of *race, colour and religion*, a teacher could ask the following guiding questions: what does the title of the play, *Othello, The Moor of Venice*, mean? What is a 'Moor', and what does it mean to be a Moor 'of Venice'? She could then point her students to the OED as a way to begin to answer the questions.

---

[7]Of course, 'speech acts' are described in Austin's *How to Do Things with Words*.

OED definition: a native or inhabitant of ancient Mauretania, a region of North Africa corresponding to parts of present-day Morocco and Algeria. Later usually: a member of a Muslim people of mixed Berber and Arab descent inhabiting north-western Africa (now mainly present-day Mauritania), who in the 8th cent. conquered Spain. In the Middle Ages, and as late as the 17th cent., the Moors were widely supposed to be mostly black or very dark-skinned, although the existence of 'white Moors' was recognized. Thus the term was often used, even into the 20th cent., with the sense 'black person'.[8]

We suggest asking the following questions:

- Who is included and who is excluded from the definition?
- What parts of the definition purport to apply to the era when the play was created (the early seventeenth century)?
- How could the meaning of the title *Othello, The Moor of Venice*, change over history?

The point of this exercise is to demonstrate to the students that the term 'Moor' was incredibly unstable when Shakespeare was writing *Othello*. As Anthony Barthelemy has cleverly written about the definition, 'Moor can mean, then, non-black Muslim, black Christian, or black Muslim. The only certainty a reader has when he sees the word is that the person referred to is not a [white] Christian.'[9] While students often assume that words in dictionaries have stable meanings (you click on a dictionary app and there is the meaning), the OED exists because language is dynamic and changes over time. In fact, the OED's definition of 'Moor' reveals how thorny and tortured language usage is for *race, colour and religion* (the chosen frame).

The universal and the relevant

There are two problematic, and related, claims for the value of studying Shakespeare: claims for the texts' universality and assumptions about their relevance. Frequently, when teachers are wedded to the notion of Shakespeare's universality, they treat the 400-year-old gap between the writing of the plays and their teaching of them as effortlessly bridgeable. There is no gap when one espouses a belief in a text's universality. Yet,

[8]OED definition for Moor.
[9]Barthelemy, *Black Face, Maligned Race: The Representation of Blacks in English Drama from Shakespeare to Southerne*, 7.

it seems worthwhile to ask: is it possible to make universal claims about jealousy from *Othello*? Obviously, the phrase 'the green-eyed monster' has become a cliché, but does that mean that Iago could deceive anyone (3.3.168)? What fascinating details and contexts are lost when Othello is just another jealous husband? Claims to universality erase history. As will become clear (see Chapter 5), we advocate keeping multiple histories in play when decoding Shakespeare's complex language. This does not mean that we value Shakespeare's texts any less because we reject facile claims about their universality; rather, the text's value comes in the rich and fascinating juxtaposition of histories, contexts, rhetoric and aesthetic theories. Shakespeare's texts get more complex over time because of the layering of meaning.

The other problematic assumption about the value of studying Shakespeare results from a belief that students are motivated by superficial relevance. In this approach, teachers assume that students only learn from texts that speak directly to the specificities of their lives. For example, a teacher may ask her female students to relate to *Othello* by asking if they have ever dated a young man of whom their father does not approve. There are a number of problems in this approach. First, whither the language? In fact, Brabantio's language makes it clear that he constructs a common cause with Othello against Desdemona ('Look to her, Moor, if thou hast eyes to see: / She has deceived her father, and may thee' [1.3.293–4]). Second, what assumptions is this teacher making about her female students' sexuality (the teacher may as well ask if students have made the 'beast with two backs' [1.1.115])? And LGBTQ students are left out if they cannot relate. And third, are we just going to ignore what 'Moor' means in terms of difference? Is it even possible to address the term 'Moor' through the lens of 'relating'? If universality erases history, relevance erases the text. We value Shakespeare's texts precisely because they illuminate the difficult correspondences between the specific language of the characters and the specific lives of students. We believe that Shakespeare's texts gain complexity over time because of the accrual of and fissures in meaning.

Collaborative meaning making

There are at least three ways to think about collaborative approaches to Shakespeare's language in instructional design: teacher and student, students together, and the student and the text. In a student-centred classroom, advanced learners recognize that there is a collaborative relationship between themselves and their teachers. This allows teachers to guide instead of provide close reading and analytical thinking. The teacher is still in control, having created the frame (a guiding topic or set of guiding topics), and her guiding questions focus student attention on the text. In this design she does not have to be the expert on the meaning of every word, literary device and/or allusion. She facilitates a collaborative close reading: guiding students toward important resources like glosses, the *Oxford English Dictionary* and hyperlinks to contextual information; enabling her students to find the answers to their own questions; and layering meaning.

A rhetorically rich example of teacher–student collaboration could occur through a reading of Othello's description of Desdemona's love for him. Framed by the topic of *the appeal of good stories*, a teacher might ask 'What draws one into a story and how does the storyteller know?' Here is an excerpt from that speech:

It was my hint to speak – such was my **process** –
And of the **cannibals** that each other eat,
The **Anthropophagi,** and men whose heads
Do grow beneath their shoulders. This to hear
Would Desdemona **seriously incline,**
But still the household affairs would draw her thence,
Which ever as she could with haste dispatch
She'd come again, and with a **greedy ear**
Devour up my discourse

(1.3.143–51)

The teacher should ask directed questions about specific language in the text in order to model the moves that comprise close reading. What does Othello mean by his 'process'? Does that term connote deliberation? What are 'cannibals' and 'Anthropophagi', and why does Othello use both words? What does it mean to have a 'greedy ear'? What does it mean to 'devour' a discourse? What does this tell you about Othello's construction of Desdemona's attraction to him? In a student-centred classroom, a teacher would ask questions that guide the students to unpack the text collaboratively.

As we have noted, teachers should explicitly identify meta-cognitive moves within their close reading: choosing, explicating and connecting details that speak to the frame (see Chapter 2). Teachers should beware of limiting a class dialogue to one student at a time (teacher–student call and response): it is all too easy to fall into the teacher doing all the affirming or denying of close readings and interpretations. When students are not confident in their facility with complex texts, they need to hear multiple responses that collectively provide a compelling close reading.

As twenty-first-century learners become more confident in their ability to read and decode Shakespeare's language in classroom discussions, they can collaborate with each other with less direct teacher guidance. Students

Olivia Vinall as Desdemona and Adrian Lester as Othello in The National Theatre's 2013 production directed by Nicholas Hytner. Johan Persson/ArenaPAL.

may be able to perform close readings in small groups; the next step is for the teacher to ask questions about the details they have noted in their close readings, consider the evidence and propose arguments. Using the example above, the teacher can maintain the frame (*the appeal of good stories*) and the guiding question ('What draws one into a story and how does the storyteller know?'), and ask students to find further examples, compare them in small groups and construct an argument about their significance collectively. Depending on when this discussion occurs within the unit, the examples may come from that same speech in Act 1, scene 3, from Act 1 in its entirety or from any other portion of the play (there are of course many storytellers in *Othello*). As students collaborate, it is important for the teacher to listen actively and help students to articulate their reasoning.

Once students have internalized the processes of collaborative meaning making, collaboration can then occur between the student and the text. It may seem counterintuitive to think that there can be a 'collaboration' between a human and a text, if the text is perceived as fixed, done or unchanging. It might also seem counterintuitive to discuss 'collaboration' at the individual level, but twenty-first-century learners are comfortable with virtual partnerships with human beings, machines and texts.

One way to foster collaboration between the student and the text is to utilize the power of juxtaposition. Returning once more to our example from Act 1, scene 3 of *Othello*, one can still keep the frame (*the appeal of good stories*) and the guiding question ('What draws one into a story and how does the storyteller know?') and show the speech performed in two film versions. The 1965 Stuart Burge version starring Laurence Olivier and the 1995 Oliver Parker version starring Laurence Fishburne provide an excellent vehicle for students to exercise their visual literacy skills: Laurence Olivier is in blackface, after all, and Laurence Fishburne is not. How do Olivier and Fishburne emphasize particular language differently? How do the vastly different performances make meaning of the speech differently? While we have provided an example utilizing two film clips as texts, any medium will work (CDs, live performances, YouTube clips, graphic novels, etc.). The point is developing the active comparison and contrast of texts; this advances student close reading and analysis.

The next step is for students to create and articulate juxtapositions independently. Again, this is an exercise in collaborative meaning making because students make complex texts come alive in relationship to each other. They also have to be able to communicate effectively and compellingly the importance of the juxtaposition. This requires creative and critical work, and students need to build skills in both to succeed in the twenty-first century. When the teacher provides a model and is the facilitator instead of the expert, the students make meaning independently, gain expertise and therefore own Shakespeare.

When Shakespeare's texts are treated as living documents, meaning is always in flux and must be navigated by groups and individuals. Theatre practitioners have always known this. While it is easy to mistake a theatrical production for a direct transmission of meaning, Shakespeare's language is only ever meaningful through the reception of the audience.[10]

Theatre-based classroom techniques

It is now a common pedagogical practice in secondary schools, colleges and universities to incorporate performance into the Shakespearean classroom. There is a rich conversation between theatre practitioners and teachers about bridging performance and literary studies. Theatre-based classroom techniques offer a process for collaborative meaning making in which language interpretation is foregrounded through kinaesthetic learning. There are subtle and important distinctions between, and permutations of, theatre-based classroom techniques (performance based, rehearsal-room based, embodied, kinaesthetic, and more). Nonetheless, they all have their roots in the blending of theatre and literary studies. We value these differences, but for the purpose of this chapter we unite them under the umbrella term *theatre-based classroom techniques*.

---

[10]Bennett refers to this as the 'production–reception contract' in her book *Theatre Audiences: A Theory of Production and Reception*.

Excellent resources are provided by theatre companies, like the Globe and the Royal Shakespeare Company (RSC). In the US, the Folger Shakespeare Library has taken the lead in providing workshops and free online resources for educators who teach Shakespeare. The RSC's *Stand Up for Shakespeare* manifesto promotes three core principles ('do it on your feet'; 'see it live'; and 'start it earlier'), and the first principle, like Folger's performance-based methodology, is deeply invested in advocating the benefits of embodied or kinaesthetic learning.

These active, theatre-based approaches acknowledge the importance of kinaesthetic learning – learning through doing and feeling. By engaging directly and physically with the words and rhythms of the text, complex thoughts and language start to make sense to young people and invite instinctive and personal responses.

Active techniques ensure that experiences of Shakespeare are inherently inclusive since they embrace all age ranges and abilities. They also mean that Shakespeare is collectively owned as participants collaborate and build a shared understanding of the play – with the whole class becoming 'co-owners' and 'doers'.[11]

Kinaesthetic learning, according to proponents of theatre-based classroom techniques, enables the students to learn and own Shakespeare in more personal ways. Jonothan Neelands, the lead academic for the RSC/University of Warwick partnership, argues that the body of the student, and the connections between the student's engaged body and his/her ability to conceptualize and analyse complex materials, are placed at the core of these theatre-based techniques.[12]

We caution against theatre-based classroom techniques that are translation–performance exercises: read the text, translate it into 'modern' English and perform the rewritten scene. While this activity does prompt a type of close reading, it does not allow the class as a whole to grapple with the dynamism of Shakespeare's language.

When students enact Shakespeare's characters and scenes they have expanded opportunities to make sense of the language for themselves. Dialogues and scenes as enacted can illuminate complex language, with meaning expressed through inflection, gestures and movement. Rather than speed through a play to understand what happens, theatre-based classroom techniques mirror rehearsal-room techniques, trying scenes again and again and exploring the opportunities for meaning that arise with each hearing. As David Bevington and Gavin Witt summarize, 'Repeating the scene with different combinations of actors in the roles enabled us all to hear what

---

[11] Royal Shakespeare Company, *Stand Up for Shakespeare: A Manifesto for Shakespeare in Schools*, 3.
[12] Neelands, 'Acting Together: Ensemble as a Democratic Process in Art and Life'.

different approaches could be taken. It also enabled and required readers to explain how certain choices resulted from the actual speaking of the words.'[13]

With these techniques, teachers have discovered that students become engaged in the language of Shakespeare's plays as well as the stories. Research on classrooms that employ theatre-based techniques, evaluating the approaches teachers adopt after working in collaboration with different theatre companies (e.g. Globe Education, the Royal Shakespeare Company, the Chicago Shakespeare Company and others), has documented an increase in student enthusiasm and made claims for broader impacts on student learning.[14]

Many theatre companies that work with students on Shakespeare's plays use 'status exercises' to help students explore the physical signals of power differentials.[15] In the example that follows, a teacher could focus the discussion under the frame *jockeying for power* and ask the guiding question: what are the different types of power in the play and how do they conflict? An entry point for this frame comes early in *Othello* (1.2.10–32):

> IAGO: But I pray, sir,
> Are you fast married? Be assured of this,
> That the magnifico [Desdemona's father] is much beloved
> And hath in his effect a voice potential
> As double as the duke's: he will divorce you
> Or put upon you what restraint or grievance
> The law, with all his might to enforce it on,
> Will give him cable.
> OTHELLO: Let him do his spite:
> My services, which I have done the signiory,
> Shall out-tongue his complaints. 'Tis yet to know –

---

[13] Bevington and Witt, 'Working in Workshops', 178.
[14] For some examples of the limited (to date) research on the impact of dramatic approaches, see the Ohio State University (OSU) collaboration with the Royal Shakespeare Company at https://shakespeare.osu.edu/education/research. The OSU/RSC project is studying important claims about active Shakespeare and impacts on elementary school readers, such as discussed at sessions at the National Council of Teachers of English: Edmiston, Sampson and Sharp, '100 Ways to Teach Shakespeare in Middle and High School: Teaching Shakespeare like Actors, Directors, Audiences and Designers'. Another example is in the work of The Chicago Shakespeare Company, available online at http://www.chicagoshakes.com/education/teach_shakespeare/classroom, which was recently recognized by the US White House with the National Arts and Humanities Youth Program Award for its impact on young learners. Similarly The Shakespeare Globe Trust, see http://www.shakespearesglobe.com/education/discovery-space/playing-shakespeare, target their outreach and performances to explicitly support the National Curriculum for the teaching of English in the UK, and are looking to measure that impact.
[15] Gibson, *Teaching Shakespeare*, 122.

> Which, when I know that boasting is an honour,
> I shall promulgate – I fetch my life and being
> From men of royal siege, and my demerits
> May speak unbonneted to as proud a fortune
> As this that I have reached. For know, Iago,
> But that I love the gentle Desdemona
> I would not my unhoused free condition
> Put into circumscription and confine
> For the sea's worth. But look, what lights come yond?

IAGO: Those are the raised father and his friends,
> You were best go in.

OTHELLO: Not I, I must be found.
> My parts, my title and my perfect soul
> Shall manifest me rightly.

Within a performance-based classroom technique students could be paired together to read this excerpted dialogue aloud multiple times. With each reading, the teacher should interject prompts that enable the advanced learners to focus on the language in more nuanced ways through gesture and tone. For example, they can be asked to emphasize the punctuation (e.g. noticing the differences between statements, interjections and questions). Then the teacher can prompt them to pay attention to which words are emphasized through alliteration, assonance and repetition. Next the students might be prompted to highlight the different use of pronouns by each character. Finally the prompt might encourage students to experiment emphasizing different words that connote status (both nouns and verbs).

Ownership

So what does it mean to 'own' Shakespeare's language? Does it require fidelity or fealty to Elizabethan or Jacobean pronunciation?[16] Does it require memorization of speeches? Does it require one's ability to translate Shakespeare's language into modern English? Does it require knowing how to use Shakespearean phrases like 'the green-eyed monster' in one's everyday parlance?

The rhetoric of *ownership* is ubiquitous in rationales for the teaching of Shakespeare. We have already noted the problematic nature of claims about Shakespeare's universality and relevance: in many cases, they erase rich histories and the specificities of the text. The rhetoric of *ownership* often gets conflated with these claims because of the assumption that Shakespeare

---

[16] For an interesting take on the value of exploring Shakespeare productions done in their original pronunciation, see Crystal, *Pronouncing Shakespeare: The Globe Experiment*.

is good for every individual in all cases as part of cultural literacy. As a result *ownership* becomes idiosyncratic, weirdly personal and effectively disjointed from the text. For instance, some have claimed that immigrants to the US can become 'American' by studying Shakespeare.[17] Glossing over the complicated relationship between American history and Shakespeare, people making this claim treat Shakespeare as the key to a semi-exclusive club, mainstream America.

So, when we use the term *ownership* we mean the confidence that comes from making sense of specific complex texts. We strive to avoid the idiosyncratic usage of *ownership* by prioritizing the confidence students can gain when they decode, puzzle and grapple with 400-year-old texts and the layers of meaning they have accrued over time.

The power of studying Shakespeare's language is also inherent in its aesthetic quality. When writing this chapter, we paused over the aesthetic beauty and the surprising complexity of the use of repetition at the end of *Othello*. When Emilia discovers Desdemona dying, Othello tells Emilia that her husband, Iago, can verify that Desdemona was unfaithful. Emilia and Othello's words and lines intermingle and repeat in an intimate fashion (they split lines of iambic pentameter):

OTHELLO: Thy **husband** knew it all.
EMILIA: **My husband?**
OTHELLO: Thy **husband**.
EMILIA: That she was false?
          To wedlock?
OTHELLO: Ay, with Cassio. Had she been true,
          If heaven would make me such another world
          Of one entire and perfect chrysolite,
          I'd not have sold her for it.
EMILIA: **My husband?**
OTHELLO: Ay, 'twas he that told me on her first;
          An honest man he is, and hates the slime
          That sticks on filthy deeds.
EMILIA: **My husband!**
                              (5.2.137–45)

Othello and Emilia's dialogue, then, sounds like an intimate and intricate dance – perhaps like a paso doble – in which they share each other's lines and words. It is beautiful but it is also combative – they are not lovers. And the beauty occurs precisely at the moment of the horrible revelation that Othello has been duped. We revel in Shakespeare because he wrote such complex *and* beautiful texts as *Othello*.

---

[17] Esquith, Phone Interview with Ayanna Thompson.

Thus, for us *ownership* means that students can not only make sense of Shakespeare's complex texts but also enjoy the beauty in them – word play, repetition, allusion, unexpected images, extended metaphors, etc. The analytical skills they acquire through studying Shakespeare are transferrable (remember, doctors, lawyers, journalists, teachers, etc. need facility with complex texts), but the appreciation for, and love of, Shakespeare's language is permanent.

Social science research and meaning making in Shakespeare

We have been talking about meaning making: what are the correspondences between making sense of Shakespeare's complex language and employing sophisticated thinking skills? How are these processes understood through social science research? To describe how students and teachers should collaboratively analyse Shakespeare's language, we draw on two well-known perspectives of cognition from the learning sciences: higher-order thinking skills and socio-cultural learning.

Benjamin Bloom's 1956 Taxonomy of Educational Objectives (as revised by Lorin W. Anderson and colleagues, 2001)[18] organizes the objectives teachers have for student learning. The revised Taxonomy describes a student's thinking (about any topic) as progressing from remembering to understanding, applying, analysing, and the most sophisticated acts of thinking are described as evaluating and creating. Teachers are challenged to require students to progress through all these skills in the course of lessons within an instructional design.

The socio-cultural approach to learning sciences (Lev Vygotsky and others) emphasizes knowledge attainment through interactivity.[19] A novice learner gains knowledge and skills through tasks that require interactions with others (novices and experts). Student growth occurs in what Vygotsky labelled the *Zone of Proximal Development* because the student is expected to stretch to connect what she already knows with new knowledge.

As we have argued, meaning making requires multiple steps. At a basic level, it is important that students know what the text says. For a novice learner, translating Shakespeare into modern English is an appropriate

---

[18] Anderson, Lorin and Krathwohl, *A Taxonomy for Learning, Teaching, and Assessing: A Revision of Bloom's Taxonomy of Educational Objectives*.
[19] For a far more detailed discussion see: Lave and Wenger, *Situated Learning: Legitimate Peripheral Participation*, and Vygotsky, *Mind in Society: The Development of Higher Psychological Processes*.

first step but, of course, insufficient. When the student is asked to identify what particular words and lines mean in *Othello*, she is *remembering* their meanings and *understanding* at the foundational level. The teacher's role is as an expert facilitator: in Vygotsky's terms, she provides a social context for this learning and enables the student to connect prior knowledge (vocabulary) to new usage and content.

Students can then expand their thinking to *applying* their knowledge – for instance, as they identify *how* a text makes meaning by applying their knowledge of literary devices. The teacher again supports the students in making connections between what they already know and what they are encountering for the first time in a text. Metaphoric language, for instance, expands their understanding of a given line, or an allusion gives a particular speech more resonance. As we have noted, the teacher guides students to access information in glosses or dictionaries.

Our discussion of the moves students must make to perform close readings aligns with the higher-order thinking skill of *analysing*. Students examine specific texts, investigate their contexts, identify character consistencies and ambiguities, deduce connections to the guiding frame, and more, all in the process of forming arguments. As we have discussed, these interpretations of complex texts occur most successfully as collaborative endeavours, facilitated by a teacher, the expert within the zone of proximal development.

Students develop a high level of thinking in the taxonomy when they are *evaluating* texts that the teacher presents in juxtaposition: they are assessing the texts, weighing their qualities as related to the frame or topic and making and defending arguments about meaning based on their close readings. The taxonomy places *creating* at the top of the scale for higher-order thinking, and students should ultimately be able to create juxtapositions of texts and articulate their meaning and significance within a frame. It is important to remember that advanced twenty-first-century learners value innovative performances of knowledge, and utilizing the taxonomy allows teachers to do just that. Students demonstrate their facility with complex texts by inventing and constructing arguments as well as imagining and designing presentations of these arguments.

Collaborative meaning making activities: *Othello*

As we laid out in Chapter 1, each chapter of this book features a section on twenty-first-century teaching and learning practices – practical strategies for building facility with complex texts. We also noted the significant institutional and structural constraints in which teachers operate (not every student has access to a computer in school or at home; not all schools are connected to the internet; class size and makeup may not be ideal; and time is always limited). Teachers do not need to be Shakespeare experts in order to carry out the strategies and activities we outline below. We do expect, however, that a teacher will know her students and adapt the strategies and activities as necessary. We have not predetermined strategies and activities by imagined student ability levels because all twenty-first-century advanced learners need to be able to do this kind of work. No student should be limited by low expectations.

In this section, we suggest specific *frames*, *guiding questions* and *collaborative meaning making activities* (for extended definitions of these terms see Chapter 2). Every Shakespeare unit needs to start with a carefully framed *entry point* (the first portion of text that will be unpacked through close reading and facilitated discussion, explicitly modelled and led by the teacher). In what follows, we describe collaborative meaning making activities that take place *after* the entry point.

Sample prompt 1: OED Exercise
Frame: Storytelling
Guiding question:
  Othello is filled with stories, and many characters tell interesting tales. What is the function of stories in the play; when do characters use them and why?
Sample text: *Othello* 3.4.52–77

OTHELLO:	Lend me thy handkerchief.
DESDEMONA:	Here, my lord.
OTHELLO:	That which I gave you.
DESDEMONA:	I have it not about me.
OTHELLO:	Not?
DESDEMONA:	No, faith, my lord.
OTHELLO:	That's a fault. That handkerchief
	Did an Egyptian to my mother give,
	She was a **charmer** and could almost read
	The thoughts of people. She told her, while she kept it
	'Twould make her amiable and subdue my father
	Entirely to her love; but if she lost it
	Or made a gift of it, my father's eye
	Should hold her loathed and his spirits should hunt
	After new fancies. She, dying, gave it me
	And bid me, when my fate would have me wive,
	To give it her. I did so, and – take heed on't!
	Make it a darling, like your precious eye! –
	To lose't or give't away were such perdition
	As nothing else could match.
DESDEMONA:	Is't possible?
OTHELLO:	'Tis true, there's magic in the web of it.
	A **sibyl** that had numbered in the world
	The sun to course two hundred compasses,
	In her **prophetic fury** sewed the work;
	The worms were hallowed that did breed the silk,
	And it was dyed in **mummy**, which the skilful
	Conserved of maidens' hearts.

Within the frame of *storytelling* (in small groups of three to four students), examine this brief dialogue in which Othello tells Desdemona a story about the creation of the handkerchief he gave her. Use the OED to trace the early modern understanding/usage of specific words (perhaps begin with the bolded words), and think about how those words have changed meaning over time. Answer the following questions about the passage using specific lines from the text to support your answers:

- How exactly does Othello say the handkerchief was made? Who made it and with what materials?
- What is the significance of the 'maidens' hearts'?
- How might an audience today understand the use of the word 'charmer' differently, and how does that impart a new dimension to the origin story?
- Why does Othello tell Desdemona this origin story about the handkerchief?

Ultimately, it is important to answer questions about the function of this narrative in the play. Below are interpretive questions that we will debate collectively:

- Do you think Desdemona believes the story of the handkerchief's origin? Where else in the play is there evidence of Desdemona's attraction to Othello's storytelling?
- Do you think the other Venetians (specifically Iago, Emilia and Cassio) believe the story of the handkerchief's origin? Where else in the play is there evidence of the Venetians' attraction to Othello's storytelling?
- Do you think the audience is supposed to believe the story of the handkerchief's origin? Are we supposed to be attracted to Othello's storytelling?

Sample prompt 2: Walking the punctuation[20]
Frame: Losing control
Guiding Question:
 What happens when you believe you cannot know anything about anyone?
Sample text: Othello 3.3.262–81

OTHELLO: This fellow's of exceeding honesty
                  And knows all qualities, with a learned spirit,
                  Of human dealings. If I do prove her haggard,
                  Though that her jesses were my dear heart-strings,
                  I'd whistle her off and let her down the wind
                  To prey at fortune. Haply for I am black
                  And have not those soft parts of conversation
                  That chamberers have, or for I am declined
                  Into the vale of years – yet that's not much –
                  She's gone, I am abused, and my relief
                  Must be to loathe her. O curse of marriage
                  That we can call these delicate creatures ours
                  And not their appetites! I had rather be a toad
                  And live upon the vapour of a dungeon
                  Than keep a corner in the thing I love
                  For others' uses. Yet 'tis the plague of great ones,
                  Prerogatived are they less than the base;
                  'Tis destiny unshunnable, like death –
                  Even then this forked plague is fated to us
                  When we do quicken.

Within the frame of *losing control*, examine how Othello structures his rhetoric and thoughts about Desdemona's reported infidelity through 'Walking the Punctuation'. Clear the desks aside because everyone will be walking around the room as we read the speech aloud together.

 First reading: we will read the speech out loud, and at every punctuation mark (commas, periods, dashes, exclamation marks, semicolons, etc.) we will make a 90 degree turn.

- What does the frequency of the movement tell you about Othello's mind set?
- Which is the shortest phrase, and which is the longest phrase (you will know them from the in/frequency of turning)?

 Second reading: we will read the speech out loud, and at every full stop (periods and exclamation marks) we will make a 90 degree turn.

---

[20] Berry, *The Actor and The Text*, 122.

- What has changed about the frequency of the movement, and what does this tell you about Othello's mind set?

- Which is the shortest sentence? Which is the longest sentence? And how do these length changes place emphasis on different parts of the speech?

Third reading: we will read the speech out loud but only as a whisper. Speak loudly the words that you find most significant. Be sure to listen for your classmates' emphasis of words.

- Why did you choose to emphasize certain words? What were your criteria for significance?

- What other words did you hear? What words were shared most frequently? And what conclusions are we drawing about Othello's state of mind?

Turning in *Othello*

The physical activity of turning to walk the punctuation allows advanced learners to manifest a tortured mind. This activity can also serve as a lead to a deeper consideration of early modern fears of turning. In this period, the phrase 'to turn Turk' colloquially meant to become barbaric or to lose control. In *Othello*, the Venetians send Othello to Cyprus to battle the actual Turks, but Othello worries that everyone he knows will 'turn Turk' once they have left the safe confines of Venice. On their first night in Cyprus, Cassio gets into a loud drunken brawl, and Othello enters asking 'Are we turned Turks' (2.3.166). The belief in the possibility of turning begs ideologically significant questions: what does it mean to be a Christian nation? What does it mean to be human? If Othello's question, 'Are we turned Turks', emphasizes the word *Turk* (To turn TURK), then the lure of the un-Christian other seems to be one that is potentially seductive and strong. If the question emphasizes the word *turn* (To TURN Turk), then the stability of a Christian identity is implicitly questioned, and the emphasis implies that identities may be subject to change by both internal (desire) and external (forced) forces. It is no wonder, then, that Othello insults Desdemona's fidelity by saying, 'Ay, you did wish that I would make her turn. / Sir, she can turn, and turn, and yet go on / And turn again' (4.1.252–4). Does Othello imagine that Desdemona has lost her Christian identity? Or does he worry that she never had one? In Chapter 4 we *turn* to identity in performance-based classroom techniques to offer more explicit ways to explore these questions.

Sample prompt 3: Examining racist rhetoric as persuasive rhetoric
Frame: Race, colour and religion
Guiding question:
How is Othello's difference from the Venetians constructed in the play, and why?
Sample text: *Othello* 1.1.85–91, 104–15

IAGO:	Zounds, sir, you're robbed, for shame put on your gown!
	Your heart is burst, you have lost half your soul,
	Even now, now, very now, an old black ram
	Is tupping your white ewe! Arise, arise,
	Awake the snorting citizens with the bell
	Or else the devil will make a grandsire of you,
	Arise I say!
BRABANTIO:	What, have you lost our wits?
	...
	What tell'st thou me of robbing? This is Venice:
	My house is not a grange.
RODERIGO:	Most grave Brabantio,
	In simple and pure soul I come to you –
IAGO:	Zounds, sir, you are one of those that will not serve God,
	if the devil bid you. Because we come to do you service,
	and you think we are ruffians, you'll have your daughter
	covered with a Barbary horse; you'll have your nephews
	neigh to you, you'll have coursers for cousins and jennets
	for germans!
BRABANTIO:	What profane wretch art thou?
IAGO:	I am one, sir, that comes to tell you your daughter and
	the Moor are now making the beast with two backs.

Within the frame of *race, colour and religion* (in small groups of three to four students), examine this brief dialogue between Iago, Roderigo and Brabantio. Highlight the crimes Iago claims Othello has perpetuated, and answer the following questions:

- Why does Iago sound the alarm?
- What crimes does Iago describe?
- How does he characterize the criminal?
- How does Brabantio know who the criminal is?
- Making note of the imagery, which animals are listed and why?

Ultimately, it is important to answer questions about the function of *race, colour and religion* in the play. Below are interpretive questions that we will debate collectively:

- What do you imagine Othello looks like from Iago's description?
- Why does Iago keep returning to horse imagery? What exactly is he trying to get Brabantio to imagine?
- What does Iago want Brabantio to do?
- Is the audience supposed to believe and accept Iago's racist rhetoric?

As we continue our exploration of the play, it will be important to ask and answer if Othello believes and accepts Iago's racist rhetoric.

Sample prompt 4: Using visual images for words
Frame: Male-dominated environments
Guiding Question:
    What are the men's jobs, and what are the women's tasks? What does
this tell you about the structure of society in *Othello*?
Sample text: *Othello* 3.3.348–60

> OTHELLO: I had been happy if the general camp,
>   Pioneers and all, had tasted her sweet body,
>   So I had nothing known. O now for ever
>   Farewell the tranquil mind, farewell content!
>   Farewell the plumed troops and big wars
>   That makes ambition virtue! O farewell,
>   Farewell the neighing steed and the shrill trump,
>   The spirit-stirring drum, th'ear-piercing fife,
>   The royal banner, and all quality,
>   Pride, pomp and circumstance of glorious war!
>   And, O you mortal engines whose rude throats
>   Th'immortal Jove's dread clamours counterfeit,
>   Farewell: Othello's occupation's gone.

Within the frame of *male-dominated environments* (in small groups of
three to four students), search for evocative visual images that you think
best correspond with Othello's speech. Once your group has chosen images,
discuss the following questions:

- What lines in the speech correspond directly with the visual images
  you have chosen?

- Do your images correspond with the repetition of the word
  'farewell'? If yes, how? If no, why not?

- Do your images highlight Othello's use of the phrase 'Pride, pomp
  and circumstance of glorious war'? If yes, how? If no, why not?

Ultimately, it is important to answer questions about how men's jobs and
women's tasks are constructed in the play. Below are interpretive questions
that we will debate collectively:

- What is the role women play in this speech?

- Why would Othello rather have Desdemona 'tasted' by all his
  soldiers than knowing she had been unfaithful with one?

- What exactly is the relationship between Othello's fears of
  Desdemona's infidelity and his 'occupation'? Why does he say his
  occupation is gone?

Sample prompt 5: Choral reading[21]
Frame: Female sexuality
Guiding question:
What is threatening about female sexual desire?
Sample text: *Othello* 4.3.82–102

> DESDEMONA: I do not think there is any such woman [who would
> have an affair].
> EMILIA: Yes, a dozen, and as many to th' vantage as would store
> the world they played for.
> But I do think it is their husbands' faults
> If wives do fall. Say that they slack their duties
> And pour our treasures into foreign laps;
> Or else break out in peevish jealousies,
> Throwing restraint upon us; or say they strike us,
> Or scant our former having in despite,
> Why, we have galls: and though we have some grace
> Yet have we some revenge. Let husbands know
> Their wives have sense like them: they see, and smell,
> And have their palates both for sweet and sour
> As husbands have. What is it that they do
> When they change us for others? Is it sport?
> I think it is. And doth affection breed it?
> I think it doth. Is't frailty that thus errs?
> It is so too. And have not we affections?
> Desires for sport? and frailty, as men have?
> Then let them use us well: else let them know,
> The ills we do, their ills instruct us so.

Within the frame of *female sexuality* (in large groups of six to eight students), perform a choral reading of this short dialogue between Desdemona and Emilia, highlighting how Emilia attempts to school Desdemona on the battle of the sexes. There are multiple ways to organize a choral reading. Your task is to choose among the many options to emphasize the most effective way to interpret the text:

- One, two or all voices speak a given line, phrase or word.
- Echo words.
- Insert non-verbal responses to complement or comment on the text.
- Vary vocal qualities (volume, pitch, pace, accent, enunciation, etc.).
- Insert specific gestures.

---

[21] Gibson, *Teaching Shakespeare*, 196.

Lyndsey Marshal as Emilia and Olivia Vinall as Desdemona in The National Theatre's 2013 production directed by Nicholas Hytner. Johan Persson/ArenaPAL.

- Emphasize line length (enjambed versus end-stopped lines).
- Emphasize rhythm.

After the choral readings, we will discuss which techniques were chosen to emphasize the text. Ultimately, it is important to answer questions about what is threatening about female sexual desire:

- Is desire a 'frailty'? If so, what is the significance? If not, what is the implication?
- Does Desdemona agree with Emilia's rhetoric and argument about the sexes?
- Is the audience supposed to agree with Emilia's rhetoric and argument?

4

Embodiment: What is it (not)?[1]

At the November 2013 meeting of the National Council of Teachers of English (NCTE) Conference there were only standing-room spaces for the sessions on theatre-based techniques led by the Folger Shakespeare Library and the Royal Shakespeare Company in conjunction with The Ohio State University. The sessions were advertised as offering theatre-based classroom techniques that would make Shakespeare come alive, engage students and make Shakespeare accessible. Teachers are hungry for this information and these ideas because, as Samuel Crowl explains, 'The past twenty-five years have seen a revolution in performance approaches to teaching Shakespeare. Many professors … have turned their classrooms into rehearsal spaces where students spend more time on their feet speaking the text to one another than at their desks taking notes on imagery, characterization, theme or historical context.'[2]

While the 'revolution in performance approaches to teaching Shakespeare' has occurred, the practical questions that John F. Andrews posed in 1984 still remain: 'Virtually everybody acknowledges the need to approach Shakespeare's plays as dramatic rather than literary works. The only real question seems to be just how to put the new consensus into practice.'[3] As we describe in Chapter 3, theatre-based techniques for teaching Shakespeare focus on finding meaning through close encounters with the text as a script for action. Students learn to make interpretive and performative choices, and teachers facilitate their reflections of these choices. As a result, the student knows the text in new and interesting ways.

In describing the Globe Education's theatre-based classroom techniques, Fiona Banks argues that the study of Shakespeare is 'incomplete without performance, actors and audience', even within the confines of a classroom.[4] Moreover, the RSC espouses a belief that theatre-based classroom techniques

---

[1]A longer version of this chapter will appear in *The Oxford Handbook for Shakespeare and Embodiment* (forthcoming).
[2]Crowl, '"Ocular Proof": Teaching *Othello* in Performance', 162.
[3]Andrews, 'From the Editor', 515.
[4]Banks, *Creative Shakespeare: The Globe Education Guide to Practical Shakespeare*, 169.

'enable young people to make powerful discoveries about themselves, each other and the world they live in'.[5]

When we worked through the current theories, methodologies and practices of theatre-based classroom techniques, we were left with the impression that they emphasize that: Shakespeare is for everyone; diversity brings some value to the classroom; and Shakespeare might provide a good vehicle to explore the benefits of diversity. Yet the handbooks for theatre-based techniques do not offer any specifics about how to address the teaching of Shakespeare and race, gender, ability and/or sexuality in practical terms, and the consequence is an evasion of open discussions.

As we have established in previous chapters we are attuned to the learning habits of twenty-first-century advanced learners, who value and struggle with explicit explorations of identity. In this chapter we discuss the current uses of theatre-based techniques in many UK and US classrooms, and the claims made for Shakespeare's accessibility. From there we move to a closer consideration of the identities of our students, with a particular focus on how they make sense of the diversity in our twenty-first-century classrooms. We then turn to strategies for reimagining theatre-based techniques that support increasing our students' facility with complex texts. We look at utilizing theatre-based techniques as a dimension of close reading and argumentation, with specific examples from *Romeo and Juliet*. While Shakespeare's text remains central to our focus, we emphasize investigations of identity with specific attention paid to casting and risk taking. We conclude by looking at the micro-opportunities in the classroom and the responsibility of both teachers and students to critically engage performances.

Even at the most basic level of 'acting out Shakespeare', theatre-based techniques can promote literacy and collaborative learning. But with an intentional frame, theatre-based classroom techniques empower students to employ critical lenses to Shakespeare's complex texts *and* the diverse identities in dynamic communities. The potent combination of the diversity of the students and the complexity of Shakespeare's texts enables the building of student agency and capacity.

The realities of theatre-based classroom techniques

Rex Gibson's canonical book *Teaching Shakespeare* offers the most sustained discussion of the significance diversity plays in the classroom. Gibson argues that an approach that embraces diversity enables the creation of the famous

---

[5]Royal Shakespeare Company, 'What is Teaching Shakespeare?', 1.

global productions we are familiar with today on stage and in film. Gibson punctuates his argument by stating: 'Cultural diversity adds to rather than detracts from Shakespeare.'[6] Yet Gibson props up these arguments by relying on claims of Shakespeare's universality ('Shakespeare really does deal in universals'[7]), and the only real engagement with diversity *in practice* is the following bland statement about racism in the plays:

> All kinds of insulting and demeaning remarks about other races occur through the plays. ... In such language Shakespeare reflects the attitudes of his own times, but it is impossible to deduce his own personal views from the plays.
> *Othello* and *The Merchant of Venice* clearly demand direct address to issues of racism and anti-semitism, and every play provides opportunities for students to discuss problems of bigotry and intolerance that still beset every society today.[8]

While Gibson, like many of the other teacher-scholars who have followed in his footsteps, is incredibly precise when it comes to myriad theatre-based classroom techniques (small group, large group, vocal, language, movement, etc.), when it comes to 'racism and anti-semitism' he leaves matters rather vague. How exactly is difference supposed to enter the dialogue? Are there no specific exercises that can facilitate these dialogues? Are there moments when these discussions should be avoided? What are the theories behind these decisions and practices?

This conundrum was exemplified in a classroom observation we conducted in a ninth grade unit on *Romeo and Juliet* (i.e. 14–15 year olds).[9] More often than not, the students in this class read aloud from the play (not a performance-based approach), yet even in that approach discussions about race, gender, ability and sexuality bubbled to the surface. When a black, male student volunteered to read Juliet opposite a white, male student's Romeo, for example, there was considerable laughter and then chants of approval. The teacher reminded the students that all the parts would have been played by male actors in Shakespeare's time, and a white, male student earnestly asked, 'Does that mean they were all gay?' When the teacher responded that there is a difference between acting as if one is in love and being gay, the comment was made to the one student alone and not to the entire class. In other words, this moment – when

---

[6] Gibson, *Teaching Shakespeare*, 11.
[7] Gibson, *Teaching Shakespeare*, 17.
[8] Gibson, *Teaching Shakespeare*, 135.
[9] Because of the stipulations in our institutional review board (IRB) approval and the permissions granted by the school's principal and teacher, we cannot reveal the school's name or location, nor can we reveal any names or identifying markers for the teacher and students involved.

the gender and sexuality of the students in the classroom seemed to clash with the perceived gender and sexuality of the Renaissance players – was addressed as a sidebar tangent: a larger discussion did not ensue. Likewise, in the culminating assignment for the class – small-group performances of scenes from Act 5 – the students initiated discussions about gender and sexuality. When there were too many female students for female parts, there were quiet discussions about how to address the disparities: 'Dude, I'm a girl. I can't be Juliet's dad.' But once again these discussions were discreet and isolated with no larger class discussion about identity and performance in the Renaissance or in the classroom.

Despite the fact that there were Hispanic, Native American, black and white students in the class we observed, there were no discussions about diversity and the politics of performing familial relations theatrically. While the images in the textbook used in the classroom tacitly endorsed a nontraditional approach to casting families (the images were from the 1988 New York Shakespeare Festival production of *Romeo and Juliet* with a black Lady Capulet and a white Juliet, for instance), the class was not invited to reflect on this issue discreetly or comprehensively.[10] In fact, nothing was ever said about the images in the book or the diverse bodies in the class. Yet, recent social science research reveals that advanced learners are eager to talk about issues of difference and frequently look to their teachers for models of how to do so effectively.

Advanced learners as Millennials on diversity

In this chapter we take a moment to examine the work done on advanced learners' perceptions about race and equality. Studies of this group reveal that they are confused about racism and bias and eager to have open and respectful discussions about them. Yet current approaches to Shakespeare often segregate his works from intentional discussions of difference (race, gender, ability and/or sexuality) and bias.

In the US, a recent study conducted by David Binder Research (DBR) in partnership with MTV looked specifically at the ways Millennials in the US feel and talk about race and bias. Although you may be tempted to dismiss

---

[10] This class used a well-known textbook for freshman English, Holt's *Elements of Literature, Third Course*. The textbook's edition of *Romeo and Juliet* is illustrated with twenty-nine colour photos from the 1988 New York Shakespeare Festival production of *Romeo and Juliet*, produced by Joseph Papp, directed by Les Walters and starring Cynthia Nixon as Juliet, Peter MacNicol as Romeo and a multiracial cast of supporting actors: Courtney B. Vance as Mercutio, Randy Danson as Lady Capulet, Peter Francis James as Benvolio and Harold J. Surratt as the Chorus and Friar John. Although not directly related to this essay, there is a fascinatingly racist review of the production in the 6 June 1988 *New York Magazine* by John Simon, in which he derides the acting abilities of the black actors.

this research as fluff or a marketing tool, the methodology was sound in terms of the questions asked and the number of respondents achieved (thousands of young adults were surveyed and recorded in in-person and online focus groups).[11] The research found that 14–24 year olds see themselves as racially sensitive and committed to equality ('84% say their family taught them that everyone should be treated the same, no matter what their race').[12] And the majority of them believe that the best way to achieve racial equality is through colour-blindness with '73% believ[ing that] never considering race would improve society'.[13] Millennials have internalized the notion that noticing differences and initiating conversations about them is tantamount to being racist and/or biased. Nonetheless, '81% believe embracing diversity and celebrating differences between the races would improve society'.[14] Despite the apparent contradiction between desiring equality, aspiring to move beyond race and valuing diversity, 14–24 year olds espouse these disparate beliefs at the same time. These findings align with our experiences of teaching advanced learners: they value diversity, they value explicit explorations of identity and yet they are ill equipped to do so.

The DBR–MTV research found that Millennials celebrate diversity, and yet colour-blindness is actually their aspirational goal with '68% believ[ing that] focusing on race prevents society from becoming colorblind'.[15] The vast majority of them indicated that they have not had conversations about race with their families ('Only 37% of our respondents were brought up in families that talked about race [30% White and 46% POC]'[16].) We know that many secondary school conversations about race tend to be relegated to, and segregated within, Black History Month and Hispanic Heritage Month; advanced learners are not having sustained discussions about race. But young adults have 'a real hunger to talk more' about race and bias with 69% indicating they long for these conversations.[17] As Stephen Friedman, the President of MTV, observed about the findings, 'What [we've] found is that these issues are a little bit of a third rail and there's not a place for people to have the dialogue. ... Our audience feels really strongly about fairness and equality, yet they don't even really have the language to talk about it or the forum.'[18]

In the UK, the National Centre for Social Research surveyed Britons about their self-reported levels of racial prejudice. The British Social Attitudes (BSA)

[11] MTV Strategic Insights and David Binder Research, 'MTV Bias Survey II Final Results', 4.
[12] MTV Strategic Insights and David Binder Research, 'MTV Bias Survey II Final Results', 1.
[13] MTV Strategic Insights and David Binder Research, 'MTV Bias Survey II Final Results', 1.
[14] MTV Strategic Insights and David Binder Research, 'MTV Bias Survey II Final Results', 2.
[15] MTV Strategic Insights and David Binder Research, 'MTV Bias Survey II Final Results', 1.
[16] MTV Strategic Insights and David Binder Research, 'MTV Bias Survey II Final Results', 1.
[17] MTV Strategic Insights and David Binder Research, 'MTV Bias Survey II Final Results', 3.
[18] Quoted in Badejo, 'MTV Launches New Campaign to Address "Complicated, Thorny" Race, Gender, and LGBT Issues'.

survey revealed that Britons increasingly admitted to racial prejudice.[19] In the survey, attitudes toward sexuality appear to be more liberal, but Britons consistently voiced concerns about racial integration and changes to what it means to be English. Commenting on the survey results in the *Guardian*'s report, Omar Khan, of the race equality think tank Runnymede Trust, suggested that politicians in the UK willingly ignored rising racial tensions by characterizing overt acts of racial hostility and extremist opinions as marginal.[20] Similarly, Trevor Phillips, as former chair of the Commission for Racial Equality and the Equality and Human Rights Commission, challenged the complacency of British politicians: 'Integration doesn't happen by accident – you have to work at it. If we want to avoid a slow descent into mutual bigotry, we need to drop the dogma, stop singing kumbaya to each other, weigh the evidence without sentiment, recognise the reality, and work out a programme – both symbolic and practical – to change the reality.'[21]

The developmental psychologist Beverly Tatum has also researched the ways race and bias are addressed at home and in schools. Tatum argues that 'Stereotypes, omissions, and distortions all contribute to the development of prejudice.'[22] Thus, it is not only harmful to grow up in a community that explicitly espouses racist beliefs; it is also harmful to grow up in a community that simply refuses to discuss race openly. The consequences of growing up in the latter community are an implicit belief that race is a taboo topic and an inability to imagine experiences in which race matters productively. As Tatum argues:

> Sometimes the assumptions we make about others come not from what we have been told or what we have seen on television or in books, but rather from what we have *not* been told. The distortion of historical information about people of color leads young people (and older people, too) to make assumptions that may go unchallenged for a long time.[23]

Silence is never neutral with regards to difference. It communicates values, assumptions and hierarchies for race and social identity.

Tatum also addresses the commonly espoused aspiration of colour-blindness. While the rhetoric of colour-blindness sounds as if it promotes equity (and certainly the Millennials surveyed by DBR–MTV believe this), this evasion is another form of silence. Like Tatum, Michael Omi and Howard Winant argue that it should not be surprising that colour-blindness

---

[19] National Center for Social Research, 'British Social Attitudes'.
[20] Taylor and Muir, 'Racism on the Rise in Britain'.
[21] Taylor and Muir, 'Racism on the Rise in Britain'.
[22] Tatum, '*Why Are All the Black Kids Sitting Together in the Cafeteria?' and Other Conversations About Race*, 5.
[23] Tatum, '*Why Are All the Black Kids Sitting Together in the Cafeteria?' and Other Conversations About Race*, 4–5.

has been wholeheartedly embraced by the neoconservatives because it enables 'a vision of the contemporary US as an egalitarian society, one which is trying to live up to its original principles by slowly extending and applying them to the gnawing issue of race.'[24] As Ayanna Thompson summarizes elsewhere, 'the neoconservatives' appropriation of the term "color-blind" actually promotes a type of historical amnesia that eradicates the need to address and work through past injustices, inequalities, and difficulties'.[25]

In an effort to challenge the social value of colour-blindness, Tatum identifies the paralysis that stems from a fear of talking about race: fear of exposing ignorance, of being offensive and of inciting anger. The research conducted by DBR–MTV revealed that Millennials are fearful. Friedman says, '[They] feel like [they're] going to step on a land mine if [they] say the wrong thing.'[26] Tatum acknowledges the difficulty of getting beyond these fears, but eloquently describes the cost of silence:

> Unchallenged personal, cultural, and institutional racism results in the loss of human potential, lowered productivity, and a rising tide of fear and violence in our society. Individually, racism stifles our own growth and development. It clouds our vision and distorts our perceptions. It alienates us not only from others but also from ourselves and our own experiences.[27]

In other words, the costs of silence and colour-blindness are experienced by all: not just by people of colour.

The social psychologist Claude Steele offers further insights into the ways our society communicates its values, assumptions and hierarchies for race and social identity. He also reveals the ways young adults are affected by those values, assumptions and hierarchies. With regards to colour-blindness, Steele created brochures for fake businesses and asked black respondents to look at the visual and textual cues about inclusiveness to determine if they would feel comfortable working there. The brochures pictured very few people of colour. But one brochure was for a company that espoused a colour-blind policy for hiring, and the other espoused a policy that valued diversity. Steele found:

> the color-blind policy – perhaps America's dominant approach to these matters – didn't work. It engendered less trust and belonging. It was as

---

[24] Omi and Winant, *Racial Formation in the United States: From the 1960s to the 1990s*, 1–2.
[25] Thompson, *Passing Strange: Shakespeare, Race, and Contemporary America*, 27.
[26] Quoted in Badejo, 'MTV Launches New Campaign to Address "Complicated, Thorny" Race, Gender, and LGBT Issues'.
[27] Tatum, *'Why Are All the Black Kids Sitting Together in the Cafeteria?' and Other Conversations About Race*, 200.

if blacks couldn't take color-blindness at face value when the number of minorities in the company was small. But importantly, and just as interestingly, blacks did not mistrust the company when it espoused a valuing-diversity policy. With that policy in place, they trusted the company and believed they could belong in it, even when it had few minorities.[28]

While 14–24 year olds espouse the value of colour-blindness, this rhetoric is not trusted by people of colour. As evidenced by Steele's research, this rhetoric in fact sets off alarm bells of distrust for people of colour.

Visual and rhetorical cues are only one dimension to Steele's research on stereotype threats. Steele defines a stereotype threat as the threat felt in particular situations in which stereotypes relevant to one's group identity exist. Through multiple controlled and replicated experiments, Steele has proven that a cued awareness of a stereotype negatively impacts one's performance. Thus, in a controlled setting when students are cued to think of themselves as being in a disadvantaged group, they perform significantly worse on assessments. His experimental design accounts for other individual factors, including ability and effort.[29]

In order to understand how stereotype threat affects performance, Steele tested sophomores at Stanford University (Palo Alto, California) who had matching profiles for university entrance requirements. Steele found that he could predict performance on a difficult test based on how he cued the subjects to be reminded of their racial identity as they took the exam. When subjects had to check a box for racial identification, black subjects performed significantly worse than white subjects. When no cue was present (e.g. when no racial box existed), black subjects performed the same as white subjects: there was no discernible difference between their scores. The power of the stereotype threat has been shown to affect women on math and science assessments; lower class French students on literacy exams; older workers on mental capacity assessments; whites on tests of natural athletic ability; and many others. Because Steele's research has been replicated globally, outside his laboratory, stereotype threat is now recognized as a powerful predictor of performance.

It is clear from the DBR–MTV survey that Millennials have bought into a fantasy that a post-racial society will cure social ills: '91% of respondents believe in equality and believe everyone should be treated equally'.[30] And yet only '20% are comfortable having a conversation about bias'.[31] It is also clear that there is a real disconnect for 14–24 year olds in the personal

[28] Steele, *Whistling Vivaldi: And Other Clues to How Stereotypes Affect Us*, 146–7.
[29] Steele, 'A Threat in the Air: How Stereotypes Shape Intellectual Performance and Identity'.
[30] MTV Strategic Insights and David Binder Research, 'DBR MTV Bias Survey Executive Summary', 1.
[31] MTV Strategic Insights and David Binder Research, 'DBR MTV Bias Survey Executive Summary', 3.

rhetoric they espouse and the actions they can perform: the conversations they can initiate and have; the imaginative leaps they can make; and even the personal and professional relationships they can foster. So how does this impact the teaching of Shakespeare, and how should the teaching of Shakespeare be altered in light of this knowledge?

Expanding the scope of theatre-based techniques

We are interested in theatre-based techniques as one dimension to a purposeful Shakespeare unit. Our focus from this point on will be geared toward teachers who are interested in pushing embodied, active or theatre-based classroom techniques into new territory. What are the possibilities for our students to grapple productively with race, gender, ability and sexuality within a class on Shakespeare? Our goal is for dialogue about identity to be central to their experience of Shakespeare. Ultimately, students should be accountable for *difference* as part of their analytical repertoire. Increasing facility with complex texts is the purpose of teaching Shakespeare, and theatre-based classroom techniques that integrate discussions of identity and diversity add important dimensions to the complexity of the text.

1. Casting

One way to initiate discussions about identity in theatre-based classroom techniques is to open a dialogue about expectations for performance techniques. A class that employs theatre-based techniques requires time to interrogate what's 'natural' or expected in performance. Advanced learners should be encouraged to ask probing questions about performance strategies and expectations. Where do our performance expectations come from? Who benefits from adhering to these expectations, and who is explicitly or implicitly excluded when these expectations remain unchallenged? Do we want to maintain these performance practices or transform them? What are the implications for either decision?

Students relatively at ease in their personal identities may be stretched when assuming roles that are intense to adopt: expressing murderous rage in the language of the body as well as the Bard can be exhausting if enlightening. If in addition we ask them to name the potential sources of rage – in the text, but also in the performative decisions being made – there is more at risk. If *who* they are matters, when Mercutio and Tybalt are a petite Latina and a heavy-set white male, students need to talk about dimensions of the performance that meld the actor and the character in exciting and

What constitutes a non-traditional Romeo and Juliet? By kind permission of Braeburn International School Arusha.

complicated ways. In raising the questions, a teacher will need to be able to listen and react to statements of difference that some students are sure to believe are 'not nice' or worse. The potential difficulties of these discussions, however, should not be used as an excuse for evasion. Remember, our students are hungry for explicit explorations of identity.

We believe it is important to extend these discussions into the realm of casting. Preconceived ideas about what Shakespearean characters look and sound like need to be uncovered and interrogated. When employing theatre-based classroom techniques, the teacher needs to consider in advance who will make casting decisions – the teacher alone, the students alone or a combination. In addition, there should be an explicit discussion about what guiding principles for casting are are acceptable for those decisions. Will the teacher determine which guiding principles for casting are acceptable, or will they be debated and determined by the whole group? What information will the deciders need to make a thoughtful decision about the guiding principles? Readings about casting practices? Readings about particular productions? And/or readings about public debates (e.g. the August Wilson/Robert Brustein debates)?[32]

---

[32] The August Wilson–Robert Brustein debate was published in three issues of *American Theatre* 13, nos 7–10 (September–November 1996). *American Theatre* allowed Wilson and Brustein to respond to each other throughout these issues.

The predominant casting technique employed in school settings is a colour-blind and gender-blind approach: any volunteer can play any part regardless of race or gender. We understand that teachers appreciate when any student volunteers to read or perform, but it is important to pay attention to who feels comfortable volunteering. Aside from expediency, there are a number of principles that seem to support colour-blind and gender-blind casting: a belief in the universality of the roles; a belief in practicing the value of meritocracy; and/or a belief in replicating recent theatrical trends. While these principles are sound, they should not be implicit and therefore unchallenged. Casting principles need to be made explicit as a way to signal that discussions about difference are not separate from the practice of Shakespeare: they are always intertwined in theatre-based classroom techniques. Not surprisingly, we argue that no one should hide behind the convenience of blind casting in the Shakespeare classroom because the specific bodies in the classroom matter (materially and socially).

Casting models

There are many different types of casting practices for the inclusion of diverse populations. There is even an advocacy organization that works on behalf of diverse actors, the Alliance for Inclusion in the Arts (formally the Non-Traditional Casting Project).[33] As a starting point for classroom discussions, these three models are the most common:

Blind casting: a meritocratic model in which actors are cast without regard to race, gender and/or physical ability; the audience is supposed to be blind to the races, genders and physical abilities of the actors, seeing only the part performed.

Conscious casting: a conceptually conceived model in which actors are cast with their races, genders and/or physical abilities framed into the concept for the production; the audience is supposed to see the races, genders and physical abilities of the actors in order to interpret the play's social resonances.

Cross-cultural casting: another conceptually conceived model in which the entire world of the play is translated to a different culture and location; the audience is supposed to see the differences of the actors in order to translate Shakespeare's play to a new culture, place and/or time period.

---

[33] Alliance for Inclusion in the Arts, 'Promoting Full Diversity in Theater, Film and Television'.

When a teacher helps to distinguish and explicate these models, the class can interrogate its prior expectations and define its working practices for theatre-based classroom techniques. This is not to suggest that the class has to adopt one of these models, but that they should provide the springboard for debate, discussion, implementation and analysis. In fact, we hope that different classes will create entirely new and innovative casting models.

2. The text

When strategically employed, theatre-based classroom techniques expand literacy opportunities, the entire spectrum of reading, writing, speaking, listening and viewing. If we keep the purpose of teaching Shakespeare in mind – to build facility with complex texts – these techniques must be implemented to further close reading and analysis. As Brian Edmiston writes:

> When students seek only to comprehend a text extract they can easily assume an uncritical stance. However, when pressed to critique they may take up a detached stance with a privileged viewpoint: 'That was stupid' or 'I would never have done that.' ... But then I hadn't discovered the power of hotseating or other strategies used to extend critique through dramatic inquiry.[34]

Edmiston's concept of critique aligns exactly with our notion of close reading, and he offers multiple useful processes for dramatic inquiry. However, we argue for student inquiry that is grounded in the complex, diverse identities in the classroom and the larger world. Students need encouragement to be thoughtful about how they dramatically perform a Shakespearean text. Their decisions and choices matter, and they should always be discussed, analysed and critiqued collectively.

Shakespeare's plays may offer lines that some students are not willing to speak: '[Rosalind will not] ope her lap to saint-seducing gold' (1.1.212); 'As a rich jewel in an Ethiop's ear' (1.5.45); and 'O, that she were / An open-arse, thou a poperin pear!' (2.1.37–8). Students preparing scripts for classroom performances may be tempted to edit out or otherwise de-emphasize troubling lines. Teachers may want to point out that theatre companies, textbook editors and politicians have all edited Shakespeare

---

[34]Edmiston, *Transforming Teaching and Learning with Active and Dramatic Approaches: Engaging Students Across the Curriculum*, 217.

for the same reason. Especially when one has to perform lines that are awkward socio-politically, one may want to change the script. Not all Shakespeare is pretty aesthetically or politically. There is no perfect text or play script for any Shakespeare performance, and all editing decisions are political in nature. Advanced learners should be granted the opportunity and authority to edit Shakespeare, but they must be held accountable for these decisions and all decisions are subject to scrutiny.

Theatre-based classroom techniques require strategic and intentional framing which should guide advanced learners to grapple with the text productively. Once again, we are using the term *frame* to describe a delimited, intentional and focused approach to teaching complex texts. In a theatre-based classroom technique for *Romeo and Juliet*, there are any number of topics, including revenge, first love, rebellion, friendship and gender politics. The frame enables students to have a focused perspective for any given line or scene. The frame also allows them to explore not only how it would feel to be a specific character, but also what it feels like to express these lines as their own selves: that is the heart of kinaesthetic learning.

We have already spoken to the temptation to use translation–performance exercises. Our reimagined theatre-based classroom techniques work to fight this temptation by prioritizing the collective grappling with the dynamism of Shakespeare's language in performance. Shakespeare's texts are more complex when identity is integrated into the analytical lenses. For example, teachers who already employ theatre-based classroom techniques will recognize that students frequently gravitate toward parodic or comedic interpretations. These performance choices can provide fertile ground for rich discussions about stereotypes, identities and performance.

3. Opportunities

In classroom observations, we noticed several moments that could have been opportunities for discussions about Shakespeare, performance, performative modes and the diverse identities in the classroom. Typically these moments led to a type of sidebar discussion in which the teacher privately answered a provocative question and moved on quickly; this teacher treated these moments as potential distractions that had to be navigated away from ('Does that mean they were all gay?'; 'Dude, I'm a girl. I can't be Juliet's dad.'). While university professors may not interpret provocative questions as classroom disruptions, they may nevertheless fear the tangent. Ideally, though, theatre-based classroom techniques place provocative questions at the centre; they are the opportunities to create greater facility with complex texts and identities in the twenty-first century.

For instance, theatre-based classroom techniques frequently lead students to search for other performance interpretations, options and choices. When

found, students are often eager to share film or digital clips that they have
discovered on their own. Many teachers will have experienced the bright-
eyed student who comes armed with the URL for 'The Sassy Gay Friend'
(for *Romeo and Juliet*, *Hamlet*, *Othello* and *Macbeth*) and loads it up to
the class computer before class has begun.[35] Sometimes the teacher will
be aware of a new, faddish meme, and other times she will be blindsided.
A strategy to turn this moment into an opportunity is to give the floor
to the student and open a public discussion about how/why this fits into
the broader study of Shakespeare. Because many of these memes will be
humorous and/or satirical in nature, it is also important to interrogate
exactly what makes the jokes jokes: what enables the humour? Why is
Shakespeare employed? Who/what is authoring those moves? And how
does this relate to Shakespeare, performance and identity?

The student performances will likewise present unexpected moments in
which the role, character and student identity intersect in complex ways.
All performance choices should be open for discussion and analysis: no
performance choices should be assumed to be unconscious. The use of
stereotypical gestures and accents, for example, may need to be pointed
out for what they are. How deeply have the students considered why
those choices were appropriate? What is it about the text that led them
to these decisions about characterization? Students need to be able to
articulate their decisions and take into account their classmates' responses.
Furthermore, the teacher may have to aid the students in imagining the
responses of a different audience. If the classroom is designed to be a safe
space for direct talk, moments will nonetheless create situations in which
there is an obligation to respond to, or point out, what others may or may
not be willing to say.

Doubling

Doubling is the practice of casting one actor to play two or more parts
in a single play. Usually doubling is used for expediency's sake. As
Tiffany Stern and Simon Palfrey write, 'Doubling was of course a common
recourse of any [early modern] acting company, faced with enormous cast
lists and necessary limitations on budget and personnel.'[36] We know from
comments made in early modern plays about acting that doubling was
used at the time, and we believe that Shakespeare must have employed
doubling in his plays for the Lord Chamberlain's Men and the King's

---

[35] Second City Network, 'Sassy Gay Friend – Romeo and Juliet'.
[36] Palfrey and Stern, *Shakespeare in Parts*, 50.

Men. There has been speculation, however, that doubling may have been used for conceptual reasons as well – that is, to link characters together through their performance by one actor. The most famous example is the possibility that Theseus/Oberon and Hippolyta/Titania may have been doubled in *A Midsummer Night's Dream*, thereby linking the rulers of Athens with the rulers of the forest fairies.

While there is no standard take on doubling in *Romeo and Juliet*, there are several roles that could be doubled (because the characters do not appear in a scene together). Introducing the notion of doubling to advanced learners could inspire them to think about the interpretive opportunities and challenges that arise when directors decide to employ doubling. For example, the Chorus figure could be doubled with any of the characters in the play. What is emphasized if the actor who plays the Chorus also plays the Nurse, or Capulet's Wife? What happens if the actor plays both the Chorus and Prince or Mercutio? Similarly, the actor who plays the Apothecary can play any other role with the exception of Romeo. What happens to one's interpretation of the play when that role is doubled differently (say with Juliet or Montague)? It might surprise advanced learners to realize that Mercutio and Juliet could potentially be doubled. How would that casting decision affect their interpretation of the play? How will this impact their own performances or readings in class? How will the class's discussions about race, gender, sexuality and ability impact their decisions about doubling? If so, where, when and to what effect? While doubling clearly grew out of necessity, the decision to employ doubling offers rich opportunities to interrogate the text and the performance of identity in the text.

4. Responsibilities

In a curriculum that pushes identity to the forefront of discussions about Shakespeare and performance there is the potential for bad choices and significant discomfort, and so we urge overarching principles of *direct talk* and *safe spaces*. Teachers have a responsibility to let the students know that the classroom is the place to ask questions and make statements about race, gender, ability and sexuality in Shakespearean performances without fear of censorship. Even with this acknowledgement, neither the students nor the instructor should then believe that there is no risk of offence when one asks about or points out areas of tension. There will be tense moments because these conversations are not occurring elsewhere in our students' lives.

Likewise, teachers need to articulate expectations that each individual accept the divergent opinions and preferences of classmates and respect the perspectives each brings. Teachers need to make explicit and model engaged audience behaviour. This prepares students to be literate as viewers, listeners and speakers. It will not always be easy when everyone is critically engaged; there will be moments of tension when the identities in the classroom bump up against Shakespeare's texts. Arts professionals recognize the need for rehearsal spaces that allow for both experimentation and the inevitability of useful failure. There are resources available about strategies for contested class sessions that are active *and* inclusive.[37] In a class that will be explicit about the implications of difference, safety requires established ways of expressing editorial comments and dissent, especially about interpretation.

Many theatre-based classroom techniques are assessed according to effort, 'creativity' and successful collaboration. We note that close reading and argumentation are rarely assessed (see Chapter 7 for more on assessment). If the ultimate purpose of teaching Shakespeare is increased facility with complex texts, then close reading, analysis and argumentation become a dimension of performance critique.

Concluding thoughts

Ironically, many teachers sacrifice the complexity of their student body to celebrate Shakespeare's universality. Shakespeare may be universal, but theatre-based techniques that take into account the differences among the bodies in the class do not take away from Shakespeare. In fact, these approaches will keep Shakespeare relevant because critical engagements in performances enable students to explore Shakespeare in the full spectrum of complexity: historically, politically, performatively, aesthetically and personally.

We recognize that the theatre-based classroom techniques described here are challenging to organize, enact and sustain. Choices abound; intentional framing is necessary. As Jonothan Neelands argues, 'the ensemble in the classroom might become a model of how to live in the world; a model of "being with"'.[38] This of course is the most idealistic version of theatre-based techniques. Even if one does not adopt Neelands' idealism, theatre-based techniques should challenge assumptions about being 'other' or what it takes to perform 'difference'.

There should be no *neutral* bodies in a classroom that embraces a theatre-based or kinaesthetic approach. When our students' bodies and identities are taken into consideration in theatre-based techniques, Shakespeare is less antique, less frozen in a particular historical moment. Students not only bring their modern bodies and modern interpretations of them, but also interrogate what it takes and means to perform in/as them.

---

[37] Stredder, *The North Face of Shakespeare: Activities for Teaching the Plays*, pages 26–32, provides a very useful description of the necessity of physical as well as emotional safety in the active Shakespeare classroom.

[38] Neelands, 'Acting Together: Ensemble as a Democratic Process in Art and Life', 175.

Exercises that explore identity:
Romeo and Juliet

As we laid out in Chapter 1, each chapter of this book features a section on twenty-first-century teaching and learning practices – practical strategies for building facility with complex texts. We also noted the significant institutional and structural constraints in which teachers operate (not every student has access to a computer in school or home; not all schools are connected to the internet; class size and makeup may not be ideal; and time is always limited). Teachers do not need to be Shakespeare experts in order to carry out the strategies and activities we outline below. We do expect, however, that a teacher will know her students and adapt the strategies and activities as necessary. We have not predetermined strategies and activities by imagined student ability levels because all twenty-first-century advanced learners need to be able to do this kind of work. No students should be limited by low expectations.

Our goal is for dialogues about identity to be central to an advanced learner's experience of Shakespeare. Ultimately, students should be accountable for *difference* as part of their analytical repertoire. Some Shakespeare plays propel conversation about identity (think, for example, about *Othello* and *Merchant of Venice*). We have specifically chosen *Romeo and Juliet* because the ubiquitous interpretation of the play as a Universal Romance often forestalls discussions about identity. The exercises that follow are intended to challenge advanced learners to interrogate their assumptions and expand their horizons of expectation.

In this section, we suggest specific *frames*, *guiding questions* and *activities that explore identity* (for extended definitions of these terms see Chapter 2). Every Shakespeare unit needs to start with a carefully framed *entry point* (the first portion of text that will be unpacked through close reading and facilitated discussion, explicitly modelled and led by the teacher). In what follows we describe student-centred activities that take place *after* the entry point. We expect teachers will need to play an active role in creating safe spaces in the classroom to address issues in identity that arise from the text. We also expect teachers to promote explicit talk about identity.

Sample prompt 1: Casting famous people
Frame: Gender and the performance of love
Guiding question:
   How are true lovers supposed to act and look? How does gender impact the performance of love?
Sample text: *Romeo and Juliet* 2.2.85–115

JULIET:	Thou knowest the mask of night is on my face,
	Else would a maiden blush bepaint my cheek
	For that which thou hast heard me speak tonight.
	Fain would I dwell on form, fain, fain deny
	What I have spoke; but farewell, compliment.
	Dost thou love me? I know thou wilt say 'Ay',
	And I will take thy word; yet, if thou swear'st,
	Thou mayst prove false. At lovers' perjuries,
	They say, Jove laughs. O gentle Romeo,
	If thou dost love, pronounce it faithfully,
	Or if thou think'st I am too quickly won,
	I'll frown and be perverse and say thee nay,
	So thou wilt woo, but else not for the world.
	In truth, fair Montague, I am too fond,
	And therefore thou mayst think my haviour light.
	But trust me, gentleman, I'll prove more true
	Than those that have more cunning to be strange.
	I should have been more strange, I must confess,
	But that thou overheard'st, ere I was ware,
	My true-love passion. Therefore pardon me,
	And not impute this yielding to light love,
	Which the dark night hath so discovered.
ROMEO:	Lady, by yonder blessed moon I vow,
	That tips with silver all these fruit-tree tops –
JULIET:	O swear not by the moon, th'inconstant moon,
	That monthly changes in her circled orb,
	Lest that thy love prove likewise variable.
ROMEO:	What shall I swear by?
JULIET:	Do not swear at all,
	Or if thou wilt, swear by thy gracious self,
	Which is the god of my idolatry,
	And I'll believe thee.

Within the frame of *gender and the performance of love* (with a partner or in small groups), cast the dialogue between Romeo and Juliet using the most famous public figures you can imagine (e.g. Harry Styles, Taylor Swift, Ryan Higa, Lena Dunham, Chris Brown, Demi Lovato, etc.). It is important to pick celebrities that are easily identifiable and recognizable by your classmates (e.g. the more famous the better). You should use the following questions to help prompt your casting, and you will be expected to report to the class how you answer these questions:

- How does what you know about this famous person's public persona correspond to Romeo and Juliet in this scene?
- What lines are easiest to imagine these public figures saying and why?
- What lines seem out of character for the public persona of these famous people and why?

Ultimately, it is important to answer questions about how true lovers are supposed to act and look. Below are interpretive questions that we will debate collectively:

- Who is doing the wooing in this scene?
- How does Juliet say wooing is supposed to work?
- Does Romeo really understand what Juliet is saying?

After this discussion, we will interrogate some of our own assumptions about how love is supposed to be played. For example, it is common to cast Romeo and Juliet as being from two different groups (e.g. different classes, ethnicities, religions and races). Did anyone cast Romeo and Juliet as being from two different races? If not, how did you imagine the differences between the families?

Sample prompt 2: Images of friendship
Frame: Male friendships
Guiding question:

How do the male characters perform friendship in the play? Is male friendship constructed as a competition?
Sample text: *Romeo and Juliet* 2.4.70–90

MERCUTIO:	Nay, if our wits run the wild goose chase, I am done, for thou hast more of the wild goose in one of thy wits than, I am sure, I have in my whole five. Was I with you there for the goose?
ROMEO:	Thou wast never with me for anything, when thou wast not there for the goose.
MERCUTIO:	I will bite thee by the ear for that jest.
ROMEO:	Nay, good goose, bite not.
MERCUTIO:	Thy wit is a very bitter sweeting, it is a most sharp sauce.
ROMEO:	And is it not then well served in to a sweet goose?
MERCUTIO:	O here's a wit of cheveril, that stretches from an inch narrow to an ell broad.
ROMEO:	I stretch it out for that word 'broad' which, added to the goose, proves thee far and wide – a broad goose.
MERCUTIO:	Why, is not this better now than groaning for love? Now art thou sociable, now art thou Romeo, now art thou what thou art, by art as well as by nature, for this drivelling love is like a great natural that runs lolling up and down to hide his bauble in a hole.
BENVOLIO:	Stop there, stop there!

Harold Perrineau as Mercutio and Leonardo DiCaprio as Romeo in Baz Luhrmann's 1996 film Romeo + Juliet.

Within the frame of *male friendships* (with a partner or in small groups), highlight the phrases in the dialogue between Romeo, Mercutio and Benvolio that characterize their friendship. Then look for images of male friendship (literally, you can search under 'male friends' in Google Images) and find ones that correspond best with your interpretation of this dialogue. You should use the following questions to help prompt your image selection, and you will be expected to report to the class how you answer these questions:

- Who's the 'goose'? And how does your interpretation inform the images you selected?
- What does it mean to be 'sociable' in Mercutio's mind? And how does your interpretation inform the images you selected?
- What is Benvolio's role in the threesome? And how does your interpretation inform the images you selected?

Ultimately, it is important to answer questions about how male characters perform friendship in the play. Below are interpretive questions that we will debate collectively:

- There are a lot of sexual puns in this dialogue. How does male friendship navigate the threat that one of the gang will break off due to love?
- What are the ways that these men understand loyalty? Is it in contrast or competition with something else?

Sample prompt 3: Cross-gender casting
Frame: Comedy?
Guiding question:
   How does humour work in *Romeo and Juliet*? Where is it employed and by whom?
Sample text: *Romeo and Juliet* 1.1.18–61

GREGORY:	The quarrel is between our masters and us their men.
SAMSON:	'Tis all one. I will show myself a tyrant: when I have fought with the men, I will be civil with the maids, I will cut off their heads.
GREGORY:	The heads of the maids?
SAMSON:	Ay, the heads of the maids, or their maidenheads, take it in what sense thou wilt.
GREGORY:	They must take it in sense that feel it.
SAMSON:	Me they shall feel while I am able to stand, and 'tis known I am a pretty piece of flesh.
GREGORY:	'Tis well thou art not fish; if thou hadst, thou hadst been poor john. Draw thy tool, here comes of the house of Montagues.

   [*Enter two other Servingmen, one of them Abraham, of the house of Montague.*]

SAMSON:	My naked weapon is out. Quarrel, I will back thee.
GREGORY:	How, turn thy back and run?
SAMSON:	Fear me not.
GREGORY:	No, marry, I fear thee!
SAMSON:	Let us take the law of our sides; let them begin.
GREGORY:	I will frown as I pass by and let them take it as they list.
SAMSON:	Nay, as they dare. I will bite my thumb at them, which is disgrace to them if they bear it.
ABRAHAM:	Do you bite your thumb at us, sir?
SAMSON:	I do bite my thumb, sir.
ABRAHAM:	Do you bite your thumb at us, sir?
SAMSON:	[*aside to Gregory*] Is the law of our side if I say 'Ay'?
GREGORY:	[*aside to Samson*] No.
SAMSON:	No, sir, I do not bite my thumb at you, sir, but I bite my thumb, sir.
GREGORY:	Do you quarrel, sir?
ABRAHAM:	Quarrel, sir? No, sir.
SAMSON:	But if you do, sir, I am for you. I serve as good a man as you.
ABRAHAM:	No better.
SAMSON:	Well, sir

   [*Enter Benvolio.*]

GREGORY: [*aside to Samson*] Say 'better'. Here comes one of my
              master's kinsmen.
SAMSON: Yes, better, sir.
ABRAHAM: You lie.
SAMSON: Draw if you be men. Gregory, remember thy washing
              blow. [*They fight.*]

Within the frame of *comedy* (in groups of three to four students), you will
carefully analyse the rhetoric of this scene by preparing to stage it. Samson
must be performed by a girl/woman. As you work through the scene,
consider the following questions:

- Is Samson still a male character even though played by a girl/
  woman?
- Is Samson now a female character? If so, is she girly, butch or
  something in between?

You have the option to edit the script to fit your casting decisions, but
you will need to justify these decisions to your classmates. Ultimately, it
is important to answer questions about how, when and by whom humour
is employed in this tragedy. Below are interpretive questions that we will
debate collectively:

- Although there is a lot of joking among the male characters in
  Romeo and Juliet, Juliet does not have any female friends with
  whom she jokes. How would cross-gender casting change the way
  humour is presented in the play?
- There are a lot of sexual puns in this dialogue. Are women, or
  being like a woman, always the punch line? If so, what does this tell
  us about the society depicted?

Sample prompt 4: Tableaux
Frame: Gender roles
Guiding question:
What are the explicit and implicit gender norms in this society, and how are they taught to the young?
Sample Text: *Romeo and Juliet* 3.3.81–112

NURSE:	O holy Friar, O, tell me, holy Friar,
	Where is my lady's lord, where's Romeo?
FR LAURENCE:	There on the ground, with his own tears made drunk.
NURSE:	O, he is even in my mistress' case,
	Just in her case. O woeful sympathy,
	Piteous predicament! Even so lies she,
	Blubbering and weeping, weeping and blubbering.
	Stand up, stand up, stand an you be a man.
	For Juliet's sake, for her sake, rise and stand!
	Why should you fall into so deep an O?

[Romeo rises.]

ROMEO:	Nurse –
NURSE:	Ah, sir, ah, sir, death's the end of all.
ROMEO:	Speakest thou of Juliet? How is it with her?
	Doth not she think me an old murderer,
	Now I have stained the childhood of our joy
	With blood removed but little from her own?
	Where is she, and how doth she, and what says
	My concealed lady to our cancelled love?
NURSE:	O, she says nothing, sir, but weeps and weeps,
	And now falls on her bed, and then starts up,
	And Tybalt calls, and then on Romeo cries,
	And then down falls again.
ROMEO:	As if that name,
	Shot from the deadly level of a gun,
	Did murder her, as that name's cursed hand
	Murdered her kinsman. O, tell me, Friar, tell me,
	In what vile part of this anatomy
	Doth my name lodge? Tell me, that I may sack
	The hateful mansion.

[He offers to stab himself, and Nurse snatches the dagger away.]

FR LAURENCE:	Hold thy desperate hand!
	Art thou a man? Thy form cries out thou art.
	Thy tears are womanish, thy wild acts denote
	The unreasonable fury of a beast.
	Unseemly woman in a seeming man,
	And ill-beseeming beast in seeming both!

Within the frame of *gender roles* (in groups of three to five students), you will carefully analyse this dialogue in order to create three *tableaux vivant*. Tableaux are silent 'snapshots' or poses created by the group – individuals stand, sit, lay prone and are caught mid-gesture – to illustrate how Romeo, the Nurse and Friar Laurence perceive the appropriate posture or bearing of a man and a woman. Each group pose should embody the contrasting perspectives of Romeo, the Nurse or Friar Laurence. You should use the following questions to help you think about the images that you create:

- How is Romeo imagining his 'concealed lady'? He says that he has 'stained the childhood of our joy'; so how exactly does he imagine that Juliet should look?
- How does the Nurse's characterization of Juliet in mourning contrast with what she thinks Romeo should be doing? Why is it so important to her that Romeo stand?
- How does Friar Laurence characterize Romeo's movement to stab himself?

After you perform your tableaux, and witness those created by the others in the class, it is important to answer questions about how desperate and sad men and women are supposed to act and look. Below are interpretive questions that we will debate collectively:

- Who is supposed to be made helpless by the events that have transpired?
- From whom is Romeo taking his behavioural cues?
- To what extent are the Nurse and Friar Laurence appropriate gender models for Romeo and Juliet?

After this discussion, we will interrogate some of our own assumptions about how men and women are supposed to act when they are in desperate trouble. Who is supposed to guide them or model appropriate behaviour for them?

Sample prompt 5: Crafting a director's script
Frame: Obedience
Guiding question:
The young lovers in *Romeo and Juliet* obviously break from their families to wed. But what are the costs and benefits of obedience and rebellion?
Sample text: *Romeo and Juliet* 3.5.137–96

CAPULET:	How now, wife,
	Have you delivered to her our decree?
CAP.'S WIFE:	Ay, sir, but she will none, she gives you thanks.
	I would the fool were married to her grave.
CAPULET:	Soft, take me with you, take me with you, wife.
	How will she none? Doth she not give us thanks?
	Is she not proud? Doth she not count her blessed,
	Unworthy as she is, that we have wrought
	So worthy a gentleman to be her bride?
JULIET:	Not proud you have, but thankful that you have.
	Proud can I never be of what I hate,
	But thankful even for hate that is meant love.
CAPULET:	How, how, how, how, chopped logic? What is this?
	'Proud' and 'I thank you', and 'I thank you not',
	And yet 'not proud'? Mistress minion, you,
	Thank me no thankings nor proud me no prouds,
	But fettle your fine joints 'gainst Thursday next
	To go with Paris to Saint Peter's church,
	Or I will drag thee on a hurdle thither.
	Out, you green-sickness carrion! Out, you baggage,
	You tallow-face!
CAP.'S WIFE:	Fie, fie, what, are you mad?
JULIET:	Good father, I beseech you on my knees
	Hear me with patience but to speak a word.
[She kneels down.]	
CAPULET:	Hang thee, young baggage, disobedient wretch!
	I tell thee what: get thee to church a' Thursday
	Or never after look me in the face.
	Speak not, reply not, do not answer me.
	My fingers itch. Wife, we scarce thought us blessed
	That God had lent us but this only child,
	But now I see this one is one too much,
	And that we have a curse in having her.
	Out on her, hilding!
NURSE:	God in heaven bless her!
	You are to blame, my lord, to rate her so.
CAPULET:	And why, my Lady Wisdom? Hold your tongue,
	Good Prudence, smatter with your gossips, go.

NURSE:	I speak no treason.
CAPULET:	O, Godgigoden!
NURSE:	May not one speak?
CAPULET:	Peace, you mumbling fool!

NURSE: I speak no treason.
CAPULET: O, Godgigoden!
NURSE: May not one speak?
CAPULET: Peace, you mumbling fool!
         Utter your gravity o'er a gossip's bowl,
         For here we need it not.
CAP.'S WIFE: You are too hot.
CAPULET: God's bread, it makes me mad.
         Day, night, hour, tide, time, work, play,
         Alone, in company, still my care hath been
         To have her matched; and having now provided
         A gentleman of noble parentage,
         Of fair demesnes, youthful and nobly ligned,
         Stuffed, as they say, with honourable parts,
         Proportioned as one's thought would wish a man,
         And then to have a wretched puling fool,
         A whining mammet, in her fortune's tender,
         To answer 'I'll not wed, I cannot love,
         I am too young, I pray you pardon me'.
         But an you will not wed, I'll pardon you!
         Graze where you will, you shall not house with me.
         Look to't, think on't; I do not use to jest.
         Thursday is near. Lay hand on heart, advise.
         An you be mine, I'll give you to my friend;
         An you be not, hang, beg, starve, die in the streets,
         For, by my soul, I'll ne'er acknowledge thee,
         Nor what is mine shall never do thee good.
         Trust to't, bethink you; I'll not be forsworn.

Within the frame of *obedience* (with a partner or in small groups), you will carefully analyse the rhetoric of this scene by creating a director's script, including specific stage directions, gestures, emphases and blocking (i.e. movement) that correspond to the specific lines in the scene. As you work through the dialogue, consider the following questions:

- How do you imagine the four characters being arranged physically? Are there different groupings at different times? How does your interpretation of the scene inform the blocking you outline?
- Who is being addressed when a character is speaking (e.g. who is Capulet's Wife addressing when she says, 'Fie, fie, what, are you mad?')? How does your interpretation of the scene inform your interpretation of the characters?

You will report and justify your director's script to your classmates.

Ultimately, it is important to answer questions about the costs and benefits of obedience and rebellion. Below are interpretive questions that we will debate collectively:

- While it is clear that Romeo and Juliet are disobeying their families in order to unite, whom exactly are they breaking from? Are all their family members and friends the same, or are there any distinctions between them?
- What does it mean to want to rebel against the establishment? What is the establishment for?

5

History: What time are you thinking about?

Many teachers celebrate the fact that teaching Shakespeare enables them to teach history as well as literature. When surveyed about the relevance of teaching Shakespeare, American teachers declared, 'Shakespeare plays are relevant because of the history one can tie into his plays'; 'I believe Shakespeare takes an amazing stance on historical events while providing outstanding psychological insights'; 'The plays enrich students' understanding of language development, [and] the historical connections provide additional background for students to use throughout their academic life'; and 'Excellent instruction for vocabulary, historical content, and the list goes on.'

In the UK, the history of William Shakespeare and his life as a citizen of Stratford-upon-Avon are important facets of cultural heritage. At the Shakespeare Birthplace Trust the youngest students are encouraged to discover his home, his clothes, his diet, his father's occupation, and to experience 'Tudor farm life' as his grandparents would have known. The university-preparation standards for the advanced learners who are the concern of this book presume that students have gone on to study two Shakespeare plays in the Key Stage 4 curriculum, including the exploration of literary and historical contexts, and possibly some work in historical stagecraft.

Clearly teachers in both countries recognize the benefits of teaching Shakespeare through multiple interpretive lenses, and teaching history gets invoked by them frequently as a means to bind together literature and culture. Seeking to make Shakespeare's texts come alive, many teachers include historical and cultural materials in their units.

While we agree and support the motive to include history in Shakespeare units, this chapter asks educators to think about which history they highlight and why. Are these plays only about the historical moment in which they were written or set? Whose history? Which history? And why not histories? In this chapter we unpack Shakespeare as a history-teaching vehicle by examining traditional models that present historical context as a guide to interpretation. We show how such an approach implicitly substitutes chronology for causality. As a way to challenge this traditional teaching model, we present a brief performance history of *The Merchant of Venice* to highlight the dynamism of Shakespeare's texts in history. Part of what the brief performance history reveals is the generic instability of the text: is *Merchant* a comedy or a tragedy? The answer to this question is entirely dependent on which history is highlighted. Finally, we make the case that advanced learners will respond particularly well to Shakespeare presented through dynamic and multiple histories, and that such a presentation can enable them to pursue divergent paths to knowledge (another of the learning habits valued by twenty-first-century learners).

The eternal PowerPoint of historical context

How many introductory chapters in textbooks and PowerPoint presentations created by teachers bear the title 'Shakespeare's Life and Times'? In terms of images, these are guaranteed to include the Droeshout engraving of Shakespeare, photographs of Stratford-upon-Avon, an etching of The Globe, a picture of the first folio and a reproduction of Wenceslaus Hollar's engraving of the 'Long View' of London along the Thames. In terms of content, these usually include biographical titbits about Shakespeare's family, including something about his romance with Anne Hathaway and his first years in London. Much is presented as established fact, glossing over the lost years and all the information we do not have about Shakespeare's life. The presumption is that Shakespeare's plays are hard to understand and unlock, and that historical trivia are the keys to unlock them. The presumption is also that random historical factoids will lead to useful interpretations of whatever play is under study.

Even if the PowerPoint moves from Shakespeare's biography to a brilliant depiction of early modern England, Venice or Europe, the illusion is that a relatively simple historical template will offer a stable way to interpret the play being studied. For example, for a unit on *The Merchant of Venice* a teacher may provide historical information about the presence of Jews in early modern Europe, arguing that Jews in Venice would have been a model for individuals who are necessary in the financial world but excluded from the social one. Students are told about the nascent credit economy in sixteenth-century Europe and encouraged to analyse the play in light of this information. We have seen assignments that ask students to translate ducats into modern day pounds and dollars. Similarly, we have seen assignments that ask students to look at historical documents (e.g. Queen Elizabeth's 1576 sumptuary proclamation for dress codes) as a key to interpret certain characters (e.g. their class, status and even religion). Many of these assignments are ultimately used as vehicles to discuss insider and outsider status in *The Merchant of Venice*.

There is nothing wrong with the historical information imparted in this teaching model, but the approach and assignments reflect a limited view of historicism. First, they assume that historical documents are accessible in terms of providing context for a play, rather than being complicated constructions themselves. Second, they often imply a direct relationship between history and text as if the play were intended to exemplify some policy or historical moment (i.e. the lock and key moment). Third, this approach represents history as stable and singular (i.e. *The Merchant of Venice* is about the Renaissance). And, most importantly, this approach ignores the 400 years of history that impact any reading of *The Merchant of Venice* today.

The Merchant of Venice in histories

The problem with historicism in the eternal PowerPoint is its canned, stable and would-be immutable quality. This type of PowerPoint lecture presents history as singular. The problem is not the PowerPoint itself, but the medium is representative of linear and fixed presentations of history. As a way to challenge this approach, we offer a brief performance history of *The Merchant of Venice* to demonstrate the dynamism of the text in history.[1] When we use the term dynamism we mean the way texts are fluid and transform in different historical moments through different historical readers and audience members. History changes texts because context is circumstantial. There is no singular context. Please do not mistake our use of dynamism for facile reader response in which personal history (or ignorance of history) trumps socio-political contexts. On the contrary, we believe a dynamic presentation of history actually challenges one to see one's personal narratives within a social framework. Nor is a dynamic understanding of history an argument for relativism; some readings are wrong (cf. Nazi uses of *The Merchant of Venice* below).

Teachers, who are unfamiliar with performance history, may want to consider the following questions when reading through the sequence of productions described below: what counts as evidence for performance history? What can you tell about the script and edits to Shakespeare's text from this history? How do stereotypes change over time, and how can you tell from the performance history of *The Merchant of Venice*? How has *The Merchant of Venice* been employed in different socio-political debates? How do you define and identify an authentic performance of *The Merchant of Venice*?

---

[1] See Bulman, *Shakespeare in Performance: The Merchant of Venice*; Kennedy, *Looking at Shakespeare: A Visual History of Twentieth-Century Performance*; and Drakakis, ed., *The Merchant of Venice*, The Arden Shakespeare Third Series, for a fuller performance history.

Renaissance/sixteenth century: Although we know a lot about the history of early modern England, we do not know that much about the early performances of *The Merchant of Venice*. We do not even know who played Shylock in the first performances for the Chamberlain's Men in 1596–7. Because Antonio's role is larger than Shylock's, it is unclear if the company's leading man, Richard Burbage, played the merchant or the Jew. While it was widely believed that early modern performances of Shylock included a red wig, beard and large fake nose, the historical evidence supporting these claims has come under question. Performance historians also continue to debate if *The Merchant of Venice* was performed employing a *commedia dell'arte* performance style: a highly stylized comic tradition from Italy in which stock characters perform stock comedic plots (like the older father who cannot control his love-sick daughter). In other words, we simply do not know that much about *The Merchant of Venice* as an early modern performance piece.

Restoration/seventeenth century: We know that the Restoration restagings and rewritings of *The Merchant of Venice* emphasized the comic nature of the play, highlighting the buffoonery of Shylock. While it is believed that this performance tradition was carried over from the Renaissance, there is not enough evidence to make this claim definitively. During the Restoration, the performance tradition of radically editing Shakespeare's texts for performance began (e.g. Portia's other courtiers in the Belmont scenes were cut). Restoration productions of *The Merchant of Venice* highlighted the comedic elements of the text.

Charles Macklin/eighteenth century: Charles Macklin's performance of Shylock in 1741 transformed the character and *The Merchant of Venice*. He is believed to be the first actor to play Shylock as both distinctly Jewish and a comic villain (like an Iago figure). Macklin believed his portrayal was based on his historical research, thus he wore a red beard and a red skull cap in order to accentuate his historical accuracy (i.e. his understanding of the Renaissance). As Stephen Orgel has argued, however, Macklin's 'audience recognized him neither as historically correct nor Venetian, but as an authentic contemporary Jew.'[2] In other words, Macklin unwittingly tapped into his own history, culture and stereotypes to portray his villainous Jew – a performance that really captured the eighteenth century.

Edmund Kean/early nineteenth century: Charles Macklin's performance style held sway until Edmund Kean altered the performance tradition in 1814. He transformed Shylock into a sympathetic martyr figure. Taken

---

[2]Orgel, *Imagining Shakespeare: A History of Texts and Visions*, 148.

with the sympathies Shylock could elicit, Kean even mixed in quotations from *Hamlet* and *Othello* during his performance of the role. Thus, in the early nineteenth century, audience members experienced a sympathetic Jewish figure, one who probably seemed extremely accessible as a nineteenth-century persona.

Charles Kean/mid-nineteenth century: Edmund Kean's son, Charles, also became an actor, and he also created his own version of Shylock. His production of *The Merchant of Venice* in 1858 is believed to be the first to restore the roles of Morocco and Aragon, which had been edited out in all previous productions since the Restoration. This historical moment, then, drew attention back to Shakespeare's full play text, something that had not been experienced onstage in 200 years.

Henry Irving/late nineteenth century: Henry Irving had played Bassanio to Edwin Booth's Shylock in an 1861 production, but in the summer of 1879 he met a Levantine Jew and this encounter changed the way he conceived the play. In November 1879, he played Shylock as a tragic figure by editing the comic scenes in Belmont and excising the anti-Semitic content in order to 'preserve Shylock's decorum as a tragic figure by denying his affinity with earlier comic stage Jews'.[3] Irving's performance was the first to 'orientalize' Shylock, and it was the first production to make the play a tragedy.

Yiddish and Hebrew translations/early twentieth century: While there were many European and American productions of *The Merchant of Venice* at the beginning of the twentieth century, Jacob Adler's performance of Shylock at the People's Theatre of New York in 1901 marked a watershed moment because it was a performed in Yiddish as a contemporary tale of ethnic and religious identity. Later Hebrew translations, like Avraham Oz's 1972 translation, were also used as key texts to teach Jewish history.[4] As Oz has argued, there is no way that Shakespeare could have anticipated these productions or this history and yet they have become very important in Jewish constructions of Shakespeare. Shakespeare was read by Adler and other Jewish playwrights as a writer who understood the plight of the Jews (notice how far this reading is from Macklin's in the eighteenth century).

Early twentieth century (1930s): There were many productions of *The Merchant of Venice* in the 1930s in Europe and the dominant performance mode was to depict Shylock as a European refugee. Nonetheless,

---

[3]Bulman, *Shakespeare in Performance: The Merchant of Venice*, 40.
[4]For more about Oz's 1972 translation of *Merchant* see Oz, 'The Merchant of Venice in Israel'.

these productions were not all uniform. In fact, they swung between justifying Shylock's hostility because the Venetians are anti-Semitic, and scapegoating Shylock to maintain the comic structure. While *The Merchant of Venice* was not reproduced widely during the lead up to the Second World War, a letter written by Rainer Schlösser to Joseph Goebbels argues for the utility of the play as Nazi propaganda: 'In this version Jessica is played as not the daughter but only as the foster-daughter of the Jew ... and Jessica performed by German actresses would never be played as a Jewess. I would see no reason why this classic work – which, moreover, in a talented performance, can offer support to our anti-Jewish fight – would not be allowed to return to Berlin.'[5] This historical moment saw competing interpretations of the genre – comedy versus tragedy – and of Shylock – villain versus victim.

Late twentieth century: Laurence Olivier also offered something entirely new when he performed as Shylock in 1970. He presented Shylock as a high Victorian banker, one who is not visibly different at all from the rest of his Venetian counterparts. Although he wears a yarmulke as part of his religious observance, Olivier's Shylock is otherwise indistinguishable from the Venetians. Their hatred of him, then, is clearly anti-Semitic because he is not presented as an outsider in any other way. Thus, the late twentieth century created a new reading: Shylock as Us.

In the end, one gets the impression that many of these performances of *The Merchant of Venice* reveal 'not history but sociology', the sociology of the actors', directors' and producers' own culture, politics and historical moment.[6] And this brief performance history is limited to productions in the UK and the US, but many other countries have produced *The Merchant of Venice* according to their own historical moments and locations. All productions are very specifically grounded in history, but frequently that history has nothing to do with early modern England or Europe. As John Drakakis writes, 'The variety of performances in the USA, on the continent of Europe and as far as Australia serves to illustrate the extent to which *The Merchant of Venice*, perhaps more than most Shakespearean texts, was submitted to the forms and pressures of the time.'[7] *The Merchant of Venice*, then, is not singular and stable, but multiple and fluid. Furthermore, it is also clear that the Holocaust has changed *The Merchant of Venice* for readers, viewers and students. As Dennis Kennedy argues, 'since 1945 we have been in possession of a new text of the play, one which bears

---

[5]Quoted in Markus, 'Der Merchant von Velence: *The Merchant of Venice* in London, Berlin, and Budapest during World War II', 9–10.
[6]Orgel, *Imagining Shakespeare*, 148.
[7]Drakakis, 'Introduction', 121.

relationships to the earlier text but is also significantly different from it'.[8] A classroom that incorporates these histories opens new Shakespearean texts for advanced learners.

Dynamic history = unstable text

Frequently, productions of Shakespeare are lambasted by critics for being 'inauthentic'. For instance a production of *The Merchant of Venice* at Stratford-upon-Avon in 1932–3 that employed a carnivalesque setting and an overtly 'comic' tone (e.g. the Prince of Morocco was played in blackface minstrelsy) was critiqued because it was 'thought that the production was likely to exert a pernicious influence on schoolchildren being introduced to Shakespeare for the first time'.[9] Reading this performance review we are inspired to ask: what is a Shakespearean play supposed to look like? What is an authentic performance of *The Merchant of Venice*? What is the best way for schoolchildren to first experience *The Merchant of Venice*, or any Shakespeare play, in performance? And what are the underlying values and principles used to answer these questions? These values and principles will reveal underlying suppositions about the relative stability of both Shakespeare's texts and history.

Many assume that a first encounter with Shakespeare in performance should be an authentically Shakespearean one: meaning a performance with pumpkin pants, tights and garters, and long swords; one that replicates popularized Renaissance performance techniques. An audience member at the Oregon Shakespeare Festival, for example, once complained about a modern dress performance of *King Lear*, 'If I have seen *King Ling* five times I am not distressed to see a sixth production with varied outlook. However, to the many members of the audience who will see this *Lear* (for example) once in their lives, this is unfair.'[10] Given the proliferation of Shakespeare productions available on the internet, the audience member's fear of a single *King Lear* experience seems both naïve and patronizing. More to the point, it suggests that students both need and have a right to receive a Shakespeare play as 'The Bard' intended, designed and produced it.

If we accept this claim (which we really do not), then what does that mean for *The Merchant of Venice*? Does that mean students need to see a production with Jew-baiting? Does that mean the students have a right to see a production that achieves its humour through anti-Semitism and racism (let's not forget Portia's lovely lines about the Prince of Morocco)? We have deliberately used *The Merchant of Venice* in this chapter on

---

[8] Kennedy, *Looking at Shakespeare*, 200.
[9] Cited in Drakakis, 'Introduction', 125.
[10] Oregon Shakespeare Festival Audience Surveys.

Shakespeare's Globe's 1998 production of The Merchant of Venice *directed by Richard Oliver employed a commedia dell'arte style. Courtesy of Shakespeare's Globe.*

teaching history because it offers one of the most extreme examples of the disparity between early modern and twenty-first-century constructions of anti-Semitism.

The history of the Holocaust impacts the ways we read the play and the ways we want to read the play. The history of the Holocaust also allows us to see that Shakespeare's plays should not be frozen and congealed in early modern history. And, in fact, in performance Shakespeare's plays cannot be frozen in that time period even when early modern performance techniques are faithfully replicated because the audience is not an early modern one any more. The Globe's 1998 production of *The Merchant of Venice* demonstrated this conundrum painfully. Experimenting with a *commedia dell'arte* style in which audience members were encouraged to hiss at Shylock, the audience response was unpredictable. The Globe's desire to recreate early modern performance conditions left many critics cold and angered: 'a crude melodrama that rode roughshod over the play's performance history'.[11] For this critic, the ensuing 400 years of history and performance history altered his ability to see the original performance techniques: instead of humour he saw 'crude melodrama'.

If we assume that we could become early modern audiences, it is still important to challenge what an historically accurate production of *The*

---

[11] Drakakis, 'Introduction', 151.

Merchant of Venice would look like. What genre is the play? What genre should the play be? We know the early modern version was a comedy because it ends with marriages and unions. If our modern sensibilities value tolerance and equity, the play's genre is much darker and perhaps closer to tragedy. As John Drakakis argues, *The Merchant of Venice* has a very unstable 'comic equilibrium':

> Indeed, in its eliciting of audience sympathy the play is balanced on a knife-edge: to side with the Venetians is to uphold anti-Semitic prejudice, while to sympathize with the plight of the Jew as a victim is to threaten the play's formal comic ethos.[12]

The tragic end of anti-Semitism, as demonstrated by the Nazis, makes reading/seeing *The Merchant of Venice* a strange and disorienting walk on the knife-edge of genre. As Stephen Orgel brilliantly points out, 'What distinguishes comedy from tragedy is not the problems they act out, but what they accept as solutions.'[13] What is accepted as a solution is not only established by the text but also the context in which it is performed, set, read and taught.

Paula Marantz Cohen writes about her thirty years of dwelling on this knife-edge, chronicling the changes in her student responses to *The Merchant of Venice* over time.[14] For her the knife-edge was palpable when she no longer had to inspire sympathy for Shylock. And the knife-edge was palpable once again when she realized that she had to temper that sympathy with closer attention to the text. As anyone who has taught the same play for several years knows, the text does not remain static even when the material object does. That is, you may always teach *The Merchant of Venice* from the same edition or textbook, but the play is understood in new ways with each new group of students.

We know that Shakespeare's texts change with each new group of students, and yet this does not often impact the practical ways we teach the play as an historical document. Let us turn to one small speech from *The Merchant of Venice* to highlight how history is often rendered as singular in classroom discussions. When Salanio and Salarino joke about Shylock's discovery of Jessica's elopement, Salanio howls:

> I never heard a passion so confused,
> So strange, outrageous, and so variable
> As the dog Jew did utter in the streets:
> 'My daughter! O, my ducats! O, my daughter!

---

[12] Drakakis, 'Introduction', 127.
[13] Orgel, *Imagining Shakespeare*, 156.
[14] Cohen, 'Shylock, My Students, and Me: What I've Learned from 30 Years of Teaching *The Merchant of Venice*.'

Fled with a Christian! O, my Christian ducats!
Justice, the law, my ducats and my daughter!
A sealed bag, two sealed bags of ducats,
Of double ducats, stol'n from me by my daughter!
And jewels, two stones, two rich and precious stones,
Stol'n by my daughter! Justice! Find the girl;
She hath the stones upon her, and the ducats.'

                                (2.8.12–22)

When discussing this passage in class, many teachers will pose the following questions: what is Salanio's attitude toward the story he is narrating? Is he a trustworthy narrator? Are we to believe that the quote is a direct one from Shylock? Is the audience supposed to laugh along with Salanio and Salarino?

When posing those questions about Salanio's speech, many teachers might help their students unpack the text by providing them with historical contexts. Students in the 1970s might have had radically different answers to these questions than ones from the twenty-first century. If this is the case, why are so many teachers still wedded to the belief that a true, accurate and authentic historical lens is singular and fixed?

A common reading that relies on the early modern context argues that Salanio's speech scapegoats Shylock. As such, Shylock becomes a symbol for the anxieties felt about the changing early modern mercantile economy. Shylock, in Salanio's view, is all too comfortable substituting money for people, and that is the root of Salanio's mocking. Another common reading relies on twentieth-century, first-wave feminism to argue that it is not simply that Shylock substitutes money for people but, rather, money for girls and women. In this reading, the ways that women are made to live under the wills of their fathers are highlighted. Is the story of a daughter eloping with her father's money a comedic one?

All these readings are useful and placing them in juxtaposition reveals the dynamism of the text. When context, that is the circumstances of the reading or performance, is made explicit, texts are more vibrant, engaging and relevant. Advanced learners in the twenty-first century need to have facility with complex texts. Learners gain this facility as they become confident with the dynamism of texts. In this way they can engage with all the complexities, including the assumptions a reader might make about correspondences between historical contexts and a given Shakespearean text.

The Merchant of Venice, histories and twenty-first-century learners

As we have noted in earlier chapters, twenty-first-century advanced learners have distinct learning habits: they value and benefit from informal learning communities; they desire explicit explorations of identity; they expect that there are divergent paths to knowledge; and they perform their knowledge in innovative ways. So what can they do with history? Henry Jenkins' research team explains how twenty-first-century students experience participatory culture. Advanced learners explore divergent paths to knowledge through intensive close readings of a particular text and extensive discovery of relevant materials.[15] Advanced learners would not expect that a single work about history could provide the key to unlock *The Merchant of Venice*. Rather, they would expect to discover and juxtapose relevant historical contexts, combining them to broaden their understanding of the text. Because there are so many histories to consider, informal learning communities further enable our students to discover, share and evaluate disparate and perhaps competing historical contexts; activities that foster such habits of learning close this chapter.

As advanced learners follow divergent paths to knowledge, their new understandings will inevitably include explicit explorations of identity. In a discussion of *Merchant* on the English Companion Ning, available online at http://englishcompanion.ning.com, in October 2010, a Ning member, possibly an educator in training, wrote, 'I was hurt that this great writer,

The trial scene with Szakács László as Shylock and Mátray Lázló as Antonio in the Tamási Áron Theatre's 2012 production of The Merchant of Venice *directed by Bocsárdi László. By kind permission of Tamási Áron Theatre and Bocsárdi László.*

---

[15] Jenkins and Kelley, *Reading in a Participatory Culture: Remixing Moby-Dick in the English Classroom.*

considered by many to be the greatest, wrote such an anti-Semitic play. ...
I found the experience alienating [because] the professor neither publically
nor privately was able to address these feelings.'[16] Advanced twenty-first-
century learners expect their teachers to help guide them through explicit
conversations about identity.

If a teacher presents or allows the students to discover multiple historical
contexts, then she can elicit rich conversations about identity constructions
throughout history. We have seen lots of lesson plans that substitute current
issues, like the 'theme of bullying', for a substantive discussion about how
identity is constructed in *The Merchant of Venice* in different historical
moments. After all, it is easier to talk about bullying in general than the
specifics of anti-Semitism and racism in different historical moments,
including our own early twenty-first-century one. And yet these discussions
are precisely what our advanced learners want and need.

As we discussed earlier in the book, twenty-first-century advanced
learners expect that there are multiple and divergent paths to knowledge.
For example, students can explore power hierarchies, insider–outsider
behaviours and gender dynamics through embodied performances of scenes
from *The Merchant of Venice*. By including multiple historical contexts,
these theatre-based classroom techniques become much richer and more
complex especially when students are asked to stretch themselves to
perform identities that they are unsympathetic toward and uncomfortable
with. Here, too, students and teachers may experience the knife-edge of
tone, comedy and context, which reinforces their knowledge and analysis
of the dynamism of the text in history.

All these twenty-first-century learning habits suggest reasons to juxtapose
multiple histories and Shakespeare's texts. It is not unusual for teachers to
ask students to reimagine Shakespeare's plays set in other times. The most
effective assignments will ask students to look as deeply at the historical
context (whichever one they may choose or be assigned) as the play itself.
A powerful model for this type of imaginative resetting and analysis comes
from Stephen Orgel, who offers a version of *The Merchant of Venice* in
which Shylock is a Latino barrio banker who is looking to expand his
business in the Anglo community.

> Latinos are not associated with money in our culture, but a production
> might make real capital out of that. After all, if, as Antonio says, there
> are Christian moneylenders who charge no interest, then why are
> Bassanio and Antonio involved with Shylock at all? But the point is
> surely that Bassanio has already gone to all the classy mainline banks,
> and none of them will give him the time of day – Antonio is obviously
> a bad risk, and his emissary is an even worse one. So he ends up with

---

[16] Steier, 'Re: The Merchant of Venice', 4 October 2010.

The trial scene with Richard Clothier as Shylock, Bob Barrett as Antonio and Kelsey Brookfield as Portia in the Watermill and Propeller Theatre's 2009 production of The Merchant of Venice *directed by Edward Hall. Photograph by Richard Termine.*

> Shylock – that means, let's say, in our American production, that he ends up at a barrio bank.[17]

Orgel's imaginative resetting pays equally close attention to the nuances of modern day banking in ethnic communities as to *The Merchant of Venice*. He models close reading and analysis in this imaginative resetting. Innovative performances of knowledge should enable students to demonstrate these skills. Advanced learners need to be able to articulate the correspondence between their chosen historical context and their close reading of *The Merchant of Venice*.

Concluding thoughts

Twenty-first-century advanced learners experience the world in an incredibly dynamic fashion through seemingly infinite opportunities for connectivity. Even though they are the millennial generation that has grown up with these tools for access, we should not assume that making sense of their discoveries is innate to them. They need to be taught how to recognize and analyse presentations of history, culture and identity. The skills that allow

---

[17] Orgel, *Imagining Shakespeare*, 153.

them to do this with a Shakespeare text are transferable to other complex texts, including ones on the internet that they may discover: exploration, evaluation and meaning making are valuable research activities. Because advanced learners can discover the changing historical contexts in which Shakespeare's texts have been staged and imagined, the plays are excellent vehicles for juxtaposing and analysing competing histories. Teachers in the twenty-first century play a critical role in helping students examine these competing histories. In this way history and Shakespeare's plays can be revealed to be as dynamic as the lives of our students.

Exercises that encourage divergent paths to knowledge: *The Merchant of Venice*

As we laid out in Chapter 1, each chapter of this book features a section on twenty-first-century teaching and learning practices – practical strategies for building facility with complex texts. We also noted the significant institutional and structural constraints in which teachers operate (not every student has access to a computer in school or home; not all schools are connected to the internet; class size and makeup may not be ideal; and time is always limited). Teachers do not need to be Shakespeare experts in order to carry out the strategies and activities we outline below. We do expect, however, that a teacher will know her students and adapt the strategies and activities as necessary. We have not predetermined strategies and activities by imagined student ability levels because all twenty-first-century advanced learners need to be able to do this kind of work. No students should be limited by low expectations.

The strategies and activities below encourage both informal learning communities and divergent paths to knowledge. Students need to engage *The Merchant of Venice* actively through every mode of literacy: reading, writing, speaking, listening and viewing. Divergent paths to knowledge allow twenty-first-century advanced learners to form and test interpretations, experiment with lines of argument and create ways to synthesize their knowledge. Through the strategies and activities that follow, we believe teachers and students will gain confidence and recognize *The Merchant of Venice* as a living as well as an historical text.

In this section, we suggest specific *frames*, *guiding questions* and *activities that explore identity* (for extended definitions of these terms see Chapter 2). Every Shakespeare unit needs to start with a carefully framed *entry point* (the first portion of text that will be unpacked through close reading and facilitated discussion, explicitly modelled and led by the teacher). In what follows we describe student-centred activities that take place *after* the entry point. We expect teachers will need to play an active role in creating safe spaces in the classroom to address issues in identity that arise from the text. We also expect teachers to promote explicit talk about identity.

Sample prompt 1: Which history?
Frame: mercy versus revenge
Guiding question:
What is the difference between mercy and revenge, and are these distinctions universal?
Sample text 1: *The Merchant of Venice* 3.1.46–66

SALARINO:	Why, I am sure if he forfeit, thou wilt not take his flesh. What's that good for?
JEW:	To bait fish withal; if it will feed nothing else, it will feed my revenge. He hath disgraced me and hindered me half a million, laughed at my losses, mocked at my gains, scorned my nation, thwarted my bargains, cooled my friends, heated mine enemies, and what's his reason? I am a Jew. Hath not a Jew eyes? Hath not a Jew hands, organs, dimensions, senses, affections, passions? Fed with the same food, hurt with the same weapons, subject to the same diseases, healed by the same means, warmed and cooled by the same winter and summer as a Christian is? If you prick us do we not bleed? If you tickle us do we not laugh? If you poison us do we not die? And if you wrong us shall we not revenge? If we are like you in the rest, we will resemble you in that. If a Jew wrong a Christian, what is his humility? Revenge! If a Christian wrong a Jew, what should his sufferance be by Christian example? Why, revenge! The villainy you teach me I will execute, and it shall go hard but I will better the instruction.

Within the frame of *mercy versus revenge* (with a partner or in small groups), identify Shylock's complaint against Antonio. Highlight the specific physical characteristics/details in the first excerpt (sample text 1) that Shylock uses to describe himself as a man who has been wronged. You should use the following questions to help prompt your discussion of these details, and you will be expected to report to the class how you answer these questions:

- What are the physical details that Shylock uses to compare himself to a Christian?
- Note Shylock's use of the pronouns 'you' and 'us'. When/where does he switch between them?
- How does Shylock's logic move from comparing body parts to a call for revenge? What is the through line in his logic?
- How does Shylock define revenge?

Sample text 2: *The Merchant of Venice* 4.1.180–201

PORTIA: The quality of mercy is not strained:
                     It droppeth as the gentle rain from heaven
                     Upon the place beneath. It is twice blest:
                     It blesseth him that gives and him that takes.
                     'Tis mightiest in the mightiest; it becomes
                     The thronèd monarch better than his crown.
                     His sceptre shows the force of temporal power,
                     The attribute to awe and majesty,
                     Wherein doth sit the dread and fear of kings.
                     But mercy is above this sceptred sway;
                     It is enthronèd in the hearts of kings,
                     It is an attribute to God himself,
                     And earthly powers doth then show likest God's
                     When mercy seasons justice. Therefore, Jew,
                     Though justice be thy plea, consider this:
                     That in the course of justice none of us
                     Should see salvation. We do pray for mercy,
                     And that same prayer doth teach us all to render
                     The deeds of mercy. I have spoke thus much
                     To mitigate the justice of thy plea,
                     Which, if thou follow, this strict court of Venice
                     Must needs give sentence 'gainst the merchant there.

Next review the second excerpt (sample text 2) and consider Portia's
descriptors for mercy. Note Portia's specific claims about the power and the
characteristics of mercy.

- What images and arguments does Portia utilize in order to
  rhetorically compel Shylock to be merciful?
- When Portia characterizes mercy as 'season[ing] justice', she
  explicitly calls Shylock 'Jew'. Is there evidence that she believes
  mercy is a universal value for all human beings?
- What would Shylock have to do to accept Portia's definition of
  mercy?

With reference to the performance history outlined earlier in the chapter to aid your search, work with your classmates to find historical and contemporary performance images of *The Merchant of Venice* that include physical objects suggesting power or law. For instance, Shylock may be pictured with scales or coins, with documents, with the Torah or with a knife. Portia may be seen with her caskets, or dressed as a man holding letters. There may be rings; there may be ropes or chains or other bindings for Antonio.

With a partner or in small groups, select from these performance images and pair one with other images you find as more generally illustrating revenge (or mercy), noting the use of colour and symbolism (angel wings, daggers) that your search has revealed. You will be expected to report to the class how you answer the questions related to the chosen text above, and in addition to articulate how the images you have selected are meant to correspond with your understanding of the text.

Ultimately, it is important to answer questions about how acts of mercy and revenge are performed in the play. Below are interpretive questions that we will debate collectively:

- What is the role of law in the pursuit of revenge?
- What are the traditional/historical arguments about the differences between justice and mercy?
- Are there necessary limits to mercy in the pursuit of justice? Who should get to decide?

Sample prompt 2: Female rebellion
Frame: Fathers and daughters
Guiding question:
   What does it mean to be a good daughter, and what role, if any, does obedience play in it?
Sample text 1: *The Merchant of Venice* 1.2.20–5

> PORTIA: But this reasoning is not the fashion to choose me
>   a husband. O me, the word 'choose'! I may neither
>   choose who I would, nor refuse who I dislike, so is the
>   will of a living daughter curbed by the will of a dead
>   father. Is it not hard, Nerissa, that I cannot choose
>   one, nor refuse none?

Within the frame of *fathers and daughters* (with a partner or in small groups) consider the portrayal of Portia's obedience to her (dead) father. How does Portia respond to her father's 'cold decree' (1.2.18)? What does her father intend to protect? You should use the following questions to help prompt your discussion of fathers of daughters, and you will be expected to report to the class how you answer these questions:

- How are the casks meant to separate good husbands from bad?
- To what extent does Portia expect the test to work for her?
- What tests of her own does she plan to devise for the suitors? Does she cheat?

As a team, imagine and then design a staging for performing the casket-test scene in an appropriate contemporary setting. Replace the casks with a comparable set of objects. Consider how a dead father today could (perhaps through a will or other legal means) set up conditions that would similarly test whether men would be good husbands for a daughter (and her fortune). To what extent does Portia perform obedience to her father/ these conditions?

Ultimately, it is important to answer questions about the costs and benefits of obedience and rebellion. Below are interpretive questions that we will debate collectively:

- What are the forms and limits of parental power in this play?
- What is the evidence that Portia and Jessica are meant to be protected as individuals? As members of a reputable family? As commodities?
- What does it mean to accept or rebel against one's prescribed role in this context?

Sample prompt 3: Locating today
Frame: Conversions
Guiding question:
What does it mean to convert oneself in *The Merchant of Venice*? Is it wholly positive?
Sample text 1: *The Merchant of Venice* 3.2.163–71

PORTIA: Happiest of all is that her gentle spirit
Commits itself to yours to be directed,
As from her lord, her governor, her king.
Myself, and what is mine, to you and yours
Is now converted. But now, I was the lord
Of this fair mansion, master of my servants,
Queen o'er myself; and even now, but now,
This house, these servants and this same myself,
Are yours, my lord's.

Sample text 2: *The Merchant of Venice* 4.1.376–86

ANTONIO: So please my lord the Duke, and all the court,
To quit the fine for one-half of his goods,
I am content, so he will let me have
The other half in use, to render it
Upon his death unto the gentleman
That lately stole his daughter.
Two things provided more: that for this favour
He presently become a Christian;
The other, that he do record a gift
Here in the court of all he dies possessed
Unto his son Lorenzo and his daughter.

Within the frame of *conversion* (with a partner or in small groups), consider how voluntary and involuntary changes function in *The Merchant of Venice*.

In sample text 1, what are the consequences Portia expects as a result of turning into a wife? Is there evidence in the play for how these changes compare with the results of Jessica's elopement with Lorenzo?

In sample text 2, to what extent is Shylock's conversion intended as a punishment? What is to be expected of him as a result of this and other penalties against him?

Ultimately, it is important to answer questions about the opportunities and risks of conversion. As a contemporary context, investigate the 2014 policy in Aarhus, Denmark, that sought to re-integrate Danish Muslims that fought, or served as humanitarian volunteers, in Syria.[18] Contrast that country's programme of welfare services and education assistance to returnees with other countries' policies of prosecution and arrest of returnees as potential terrorists. Below are interpretive questions about conversion that we will debate collectively:

- Who is to credit or blame for national, racial or political identity and how/when identity matters?
- Are conversions treated as authentic and permanent? When? Why?
- How much credence is there to a saying like, 'once a _____, always a _____' in your community (fill in the blank with an identity of choice).

---

[18] See, for example, the article by Simon Hooper at: http://www.aljazeera.com/indepth/features/2014/09/denmark-introduces-rehab-syrian-fighters-201496125229948625.html, and the articles by Faiola and Mekhennet at: http://www.washingtonpost.com/world/europe/denmark-tries-a-soft-handed-approach-to-returned-islamist-fighters/2014/10/19/3516e8f3-515e-4adc-a2cb-c0261dd7dd4a_story.html or http://www.independent.co.uk/news/world/europe/aarhus-the-danish-town-where-syrias-fighters-are-welcomed-home-9806876.html

Sample prompt 4: Performing Bassanio
Frame: Worth and kind
Guiding Question: How is one's worth determined, and what do kin and kind have to do with it?
Sample text: *The Merchant of Venice* 1.1.161–72

> BASSANIO: In Belmont is a lady richly left,
> And she is fair and, fairer than that word,
> Of wondrous virtues. Sometimes from her eyes
> I did receive fair speechless messages.
> Her name is Portia, nothing undervalued
> To Cato's daughter, Brutus' Portia.
> Nor is the wide world ignorant of her worth,
> For the four winds blow in from every coast
> Renowned suitors, and her sunny locks
> Hang on her temples like a golden fleece,
> Which makes her seat of Belmont Colchis' strand,
> And many Jasons come in quest of her.

Within the frame of *worth and kind* (with a partner or in small groups), prepare and then perform Bassanio's description of Portia multiple times. You should use the following questions to help prompt your performance decisions, and you will be expected to report to the class how you answer these questions:

- What words indicate reasons why he finds her worthy of pursuit?
- What indicates that he feels he might succeed despite the 'many Jasons' who are competing?
- How will each of these reasons influence how you perform this speech (and depict Bassanio's attraction)?
- What are the most radical possibilities? Is Bassanio evil? Closeted? In search of fame?

Your audience, big or small, should take on the role of the listening Antonio, who will decide, after each performance, if and how the performance has convinced him to lend the necessary money for traveling to Belmont to woo Portia. Ultimately, it is important that you can answer questions about the worth of Portia and, by extension, women, in the play.

Sample prompt 5: Imagining the future
Frame: The law
Guiding question:
   What does the law represent in *The Merchant of Venice*, and is it represented as a universal?
Sample text: *The Merchant of Venice* 3.3.26–34

> ANTONIO: The Duke cannot deny the course of law;
>   For the commodity that strangers have
>   With us in Venice, if it be denied,
>   Will much impeach the justice of the state,
>   Since that the trade and profit of the city
>   Consisteth of all nations. Therefore, go;
>   These griefs and losses have so bated me
>   That I shall hardly spare a pound of flesh
>   Tomorrow to my bloody creditor.

Within the frame of *the law* (with a partner or in small groups), carefully analyse the 3.3 scene. As an extension for your analysis, you will imagine and create a new setting, at least 100 years in the future, for this scene. Your setting might be on a space ship or on a planet elsewhere in the galaxy: the important idea to capture is that, in this place, notions of *law* are not shared/understood by all the inhabitants. You should use the following questions to help prompt your decisions, and you will be expected to report to the class how you answer these questions:

- How do you imagine Antonio as a prisoner? How would he be treated by, and treat his, jailer?
- What is Salanio doing in this scene? Does he comfort Antonio? Does Shylock acknowledge his presence?
- Why does Shylock repeatedly insist he will 'have my bond' (3.3.6ff.)?

In order to prepare the reset scene for performance (or otherwise sharing with your classmates) you will need to work through it and consider the following questions:

- What is the equivalent of the bond that Shylock demands? How might the debt be symbolized?
- To whom does the civic reputation of Venice (or, say, Venus) matter? How would the state, the law or those in power be identified?
- What are the relationships among mercy, justice and revenge on this planet?

You will describe and perform your reset scene for your classmates. Ultimately, it is important to answer questions about the law, society and outsiders. Below are interpretive questions that we will debate collectively:

- Why might individuals in charge of commerce want to be sure that the spoken word does not matter as much as a document?
- To what extent did your portrayal of the scene represent what you see as a universal truth about law?
- How might a performance of this Shakespeare play be used to describe/explain Western notions of law? In which scenes might an 'outsider' be most confused by such a portrayal?

6

Writing assignments
with purpose

In a student-centred classroom, advanced learners should be writing throughout the study of a Shakespeare play as well as at its conclusion. We define writing in a broad sense, including process writings such as student reflections, short responsive work and collaborative creations produced in informal learning communities. We are interested in ways that effective writing instruction can be integrated into a study of a Shakespeare play. A successful instructional design will incorporate write-to-learn strategies as well as cumulative writing to close a unit. Cumulative writing assignments are more complex and formal. All writing assignments should be designed to allow students to practice or demonstrate their growing independent facility with complex texts. In Chapter 7 we will address timed or 'on demand' writing.

Every good English literature class includes thoughtful writing assignments that ask students to be attentive to purpose, audience and mode. In order to be college and career ready, advanced learners need to be able to move fluidly between different modes of written expression. We have noticed that student writing about Shakespeare's plays is frequently skewed away from attention to purpose, audience and mode and is instead focused on the recall and rationalization of plot points, or on expressing judgement of a character from a play based on current sensibilities. We want to promote and support more argument-based writing, while at the same time avoiding formulaic approaches that ape the conventions of literary criticism. As described by Robert E. Probst and Kylene Beers, we are interested in students becoming alert for textual elements and pithy quotations that support their arguments rather than scavenger hunting for details that interest the teacher.[1]

In what forms should students write about Shakespeare's plays? Our belief is that writing (as a part of the study of a Shakespeare play) should range appropriately from the personal and responsive to the evaluative

---

[1] Beers and Probst, *Notice & Note: Strategies for Close Reading*, 111.

and creative. Deborah Dean describes critical and creative approaches to different writing tasks, encouraging teachers to offer task options, rather than formulas, for student written expression.[2] This chapter suggests multiple forms for student writings about Shakespeare's plays – including opportunities to develop active approaches into meaningful written work. Teachers are challenged to design assignments that incorporate twenty-first-century identities as a part of the work of literary analysis. We offer suggestions to utilize digital tools for writing-to-learn and multimodal projects to aid that integration.

We have already argued why Shakespeare needs to be the vehicle instead of the destination for advanced learners. When Shakespeare is merely the destination, teacher-centred classrooms are inevitable and the writing assignments are easily prescribed and the answers are available on Google. On the opposite end of the spectrum, teachers may be tempted to substitute what should be write-to-learn assignments for more demanding independent critical argument. Advanced learners should be writing all the time, sharing their ideas, using their writing for the basis of discussion and trying out ideas that might contribute to an argument-based essay; but these are process writing *activities* that are necessary steps toward understanding and are insufficient as demonstrations of independent facility with complex texts. When Shakespeare is the vehicle for an increased facility with complex texts, then writing assignments need to offer advanced learners challenging creative and critical tasks. Our goal is to support a student's exploration of complex texts through writing, and enable her to create a complex text in response.

Below we describe useful write-to-learn assignments and how to build them towards more demanding independent creative and critical tasks. Also below we integrate writing into theatre-based practices in such a way that close reading leads to close writing. We close this chapter with guidelines for more formal cumulative writing assignments before addressing the challenges of assessment in Chapter 7.

Writing-to-learn about Shakespeare

We have selected *Julius Caesar* for the exercises that follow, but these writing exercises are applicable to the teaching of other plays. In each case, student writing serves as the tool for communicating ideas that may not be fully formed or that will need revision. Like Jim Burke, we understand writing-to-learn as including multiple forms, including explication (summaries, paraphrases, personal responses), annotation (notes to be used later in more

---

[2]Dean, *Genre Theory: Teaching, Writing, and Being*, 8–11.

extended analyses) and rehearsal (shorter writings that build to more extended analyses).[3] In this chapter we focus on writing tasks, but write-to-learn strategies should be embedded in a class session that includes close reading, discussion of ideas, listening to others and viewing examples critically. A class session might include time taken for students to write down their ideas, share them informally with nearby classmates and add these insights to the broader class discussion. In the assessment chapter (Chapter 7), we offer some ideas for giving students credit for this work without overburdening the teacher. In this chapter, however, we offer writing prompts for advanced learners that will challenge and build their analytical skills.

1. The OED exercise

As we discussed in Chapter 3, an OED exercise asks students to think about the dynamism of the English language. As a write-to-learn exercise students can discover and describe the etymology and mutating meanings and uses of particular words. As an example, within a frame about *class hierarchies in Rome*, one could ask the students to use the OED to gloss 'Being mechanical' (1.1.3). While there are still some printed editions of the dictionary in school libraries, the OED is now available online for free at http://www.oxforddictionaries.com/us; there is also an OED app. Utilizing the OED, students will discover, and should be asked to explain, the early modern meaning of *mechanical*.

A sample writing-to-learn OED prompt might ask students to write a paragraph that explains: (*a*) if *mechanical* is used anywhere else in the text; (*b*) what seventeenth-century uses and meanings for *mechanical* the OED lists (students should note if all references point to Shakespeare's use as unique); and (*c*) how the meaning (and which meaning) of *mechanical* should be performed and why. The goal of this exercise is to illustrate to advanced learners that no one single definition is sufficient – that language changes with time, culture and location. As an extension of this writing-to-learn exercise, students could be asked to connect the meanings of *mechanical* with the class hierarchies depicted in *Julius Caesar* in a longer argument-driven writing assignment.

2. Translation/imitation exercise

Imitative exercises combine close reading and inventive processes. They also establish a seriousness about starting with the text – being attentive

---

[3]Many teachers of writing processes elaborate on write-to-learn strategies. Burke, *The English Teacher's Companion: A Completely New Guide to Classroom, Curriculum, and the Profession*, 4th edition, offers an extensive guide to supporting students as they generate ideas in response to texts, 51–7; 169–70.

to the details of a given speech – that should also be required in longer or more elaborate creative works where students are transposing scenes to other times and places. A consistent attentiveness to details in Shakespeare's writing and performances of his work develops a habit of mind for how advanced learners should approach complex texts: the devil is always in the details. James McKinnon describes the possibility of teaching creative and critical thinking in combination, rather than as artificially distinct. As he writes, '*everything* we do and say, to the extent that it consists of putting familiar materials to new uses in a new context, is adaptation; adaptation is not the opposite of creativity, but the basis of it'.[4]

The writing-to-learn prompt that asks students to imitate Shakespeare's poetry can offer an opportunity to play with language: to untangle not only its 'old timey' complexity, but also its poetic craft. A famous bit from the beginning of *Julius Caesar* offers an excellent starting place.

Let me have men about me that are fat,
Sleek-headed men, and such as sleep a-nights.
Yond Cassius has a lean and hungry look:
He thinks too much: such men are dangerous.
                    (1.2.191–4)

Students should be asked to replace the nouns and adjectives as a way to prompt close reading. Maintaining the structure (this particular structure is oppositional: friends versus enemies), they should explore how a different topic generates new words. Potential topics include pets, Facebook friends, professional athletes, etc. The exercise is meant to enable students to play with poetic lines and diction: not to write deathless verse.

Let me have _____ about me that are _____,
_____, and _____.
Yond _____ has a _____ look:
S/he thinks _____: such _____ are _____.

In another use of imitation, advanced learners can explore extended metaphor. In the fourth act of *Julius Caesar* Brutus speaks using an extended metaphor describing opportunity.

There is a tide in the affairs of men
Which, taken at the flood, leads on to fortune:
Omitted, all the voyage of their life
Is bound in shallows and in miseries.
On such a full sea are we now afloat,

---

[4]McKinnon, 'Creative Copying?: The Pedagogy of Adaptation', 56–7.

The cast of the Donmar Warehouse's 2012 production of Julius Caesar *directed by Phyllida Lloyd. Photograph by Helen Maybanks.*

> And we must take the current when it serves,
> Or lose our ventures.
>
> (4.3.216–22)

Students should be asked to identify what abstract concept is being described (again, this is to facilitate close reading). Then the students should be asked to enumerate the details of the metaphor, not simply to identify it but to recognize the facets of the comparison. Requiring students to attempt to imitate or recreate an extended metaphor encourages them to recognize the component parts of the comparison. The writing-to-learn prompt will give them an abstract concept, such as ethical decisions, loyalty, honour or justice, and ask them to generate a series of comparisons. The form of the speech may provide a useful constraint for their thinking and creation.

3. Frame-based questions for informal writing

Teachers working in the Folger Shakespeare Library's Teaching Shakespeare Institute have created a practical approach to 3.3 of *Julius Caesar* that leads to a dynamic experience of public group activity.[5] Embedding this exercise

---

[5]Folger Shakespeare, 'Lesson 15: Tear Him for His Bad Verses: Cinna the Poet and Shakespeare's Sonnets'.

in write-to-learn activities allows advanced learners to interrogate assumptions about who has the right to be above the law.

Students should write for five minutes listing the differences between citizens and mobs. The teacher then organizes an active approach to *Julius Caesar* 3.3. Some teachers distribute the roles of plebeians across many students so as to create a true feeling of group action (e.g. twenty-three parts vs. five). Dramatic approaches typically encourage students to experiment with different blockings for the scene (e.g. different physical expressions of threat, intimidation and dominance). Likewise, many active approaches work because repetition enables students to tease out the subtleties of the text.

As a follow up to this theatre-based activity, advanced learners could be asked to return to 1.1 to answer the following prompt: Are the Carpenter and Cobbler of 1.1 the plebeians of 3.3? Why or why not? Student answers must be supported with evidence from the text. The purpose of this write-to-learn exercise is to launch the advanced learners into an informed discussion about the differences between characters whose actions are rationalized by their backstories (e.g. Brutus and the conspirators) and those characters who are afforded no distinctions and are even unnamed (e.g. the plebeians).

For the most sophisticated advanced learners an exercise using Giorgio Agamben's theory of the state of exception (see textbox) provides a complex text that can be used to discuss current events (e.g. the US's use of warrantless data sweeps by the NSA; the UK's ubiquitous use of CCTV; and the hero/villain hackers who individually determine what state secrets should be public). Within the frame of *citizens and mobs* students can consider who is empowered to be above the law.

Excerpts from Giorgio Agamben's
State of Exception
(trans. Kevin Attell)

Carl Schmitt linked the state of exception with sovereign powers

> The sovereign, who can decide on the state of exception, guarantees its anchorage to the juridical order. But precisely because the decision here concerns the very annulment of the norm, that is, because the state of exception represents the inclusion and capture of a space that is neither outside nor inside (the space that corresponds to the annulled and suspended norm), 'the sovereign stands outside of the normally valid juridical order, and yet belongs to it, for it is

he who is responsible for deciding whether the constitution can be suspended *in toto*.'[6]

Agamben extends Schmitt's theory of the state of exception to modern democracies

The state of exception tends increasingly to appear as the dominant paradigm of government in contemporary politics. This transformation of a provisional and exceptional measure into a technique of government threatens radically to alter – in fact, has already palpably altered – the structure and meaning of the traditional distinction between constitutional forms. Indeed, from this perspective, the state of exception appears as a threshold of indeterminacy between democracy and absolutism.[7]

Agamben then wonders if individuals can act according to the state of exception

If we wanted at all costs to give a name to a human action performed under conditions of anomie [lawlessness], we might say that he who acts during the *iustitium* [the suspension of the courts] neither executes nor transgresses the law, but *inexecutes* it. His actions, in this sense, are mere facts, the appraisal of which, once the *iustitium* [the suspension of the courts] is expired, will depend on the circumstances.[8]

4. Writing about film trailers

Writing-to-learn exercises can also be used in response to viewing film or digital material. We particularly like using film trailers or film-style trailers for live productions in our classrooms because they are relatively short and can be shown multiple times to enable close viewing skills.[9] Prompts might first ask individuals to observe and write all the interpretive details they think are important or controversial. A classroom could utilize informal learning communities in which students share and compare observations in order to debate the merits of the interpretive choices made in the trailer.

---

[6] Agamben, *State of Exception*, 35.
[7] Agamben, *State of Exception*, 2–3.
[8] Agamben, *State of Exception*, 50.
[9] An excellent resource connecting Shakespeare study and film in the secondary classroom is Dakin's *Reading Shakespeare Film First*.

Students will likely move from noticing superficial characteristics of certain actors, costumes and the mise en scène to a more complex consideration of performance as interpretation.

At this point this writing-to-learn exercise should push students toward the more demanding question of what they would offer instead. For instance, the writing-to-learn prompt might ask students if *Julius Caesar* is only about ancient Rome. Where should the play be set, and in what time period? Prompts that ask students to identify specific actors help advanced learners understand the impact of casting on interpretation. Which specific actor would you cast as Caesar, Portia, Cassius, Calphurnia, Brutus, Antony, etc? Which physical attributes convey that interpretation, and how do gender, race and ethnicity play into those assumptions? In a fully wired classroom, advanced learners can find specific images of potential Caesars at the moment of discussion. Ultimately, students should be challenged to articulate the correspondences between the text and the illustrations they are choosing.

5. Finish-the-scene exercise

Looking closely at the dialogue between Portia and Brutus when she asks to know what is troubling him (2.1.278–97), advanced learners should be asked to outline the logic of Portia's rhetorical strategy. How does her argument progress? What rhetorical tropes does she employ? How does she define what it means to be a wife? How does she define marriage?

Teachers should use Portia's revelation of her 'voluntary wound' (2.1.297–301) to complicate student interpretations of Portia's rhetorical strategy. The write-to-learn prompt should ask students to outline: what visual rhetoric does Portia employ and why? Does that visual rhetoric complicate Portia's credibility? Does the 'voluntary wound' make her more trustworthy as a wife and partner to Brutus?

Class discussion should then review Portia's strategies but the purpose for this write-to-learn exercise is to prepare students to analyse Brutus's response. How advanced learners define the roles, rights and responsibilities of husbands and wives will inform this discussion. And, furthermore, the students' assumptions about historical perspectives on marriage and self-mutilation will come into play. A teacher can begin the discussion asking what students think they know about: marriages among the elite in Rome; Renaissance perspectives on pre-Christian Roman morals and actions; and twenty-first-century relations to Roman and Renaissance codes of conduct. It is important to interrogate the assumptions collectively in order for students to fully explore Brutus's response to Portia's self-mutilation.

Students will see that Brutus's response to Portia's revelation is interrupted, but students should be encouraged to rewrite the scene so that the couple are not interrupted and Brutus must have a complete response to what has been said and done. For instance, the prompt could ask: if Brutus is not interrupted, does he take out a knife and cut his own thigh as a show of solidarity and fidelity? Does he send for Cassius to introduce Portia as the newest conspirator? Does he call an ambulance and/or a psychiatrist? The purpose of this write-to-learn exercise is to reveal students' interpretations of Brutus's response and to get them thinking about performance and anachronism. Later in the unit, if they are asked to modernize or reset a scene, these are the kinds of questions required for interpretive and performative opportunities.

Cumulative writing: Demonstrating facility with complex texts

When write-to-learn exercises are designed to encourage and enable close reading and an attention to detail in Shakespeare's works, cumulative writing can be designed to foster sophisticated analytical writing. Like George Hillocks, we believe that analytical writing is more than persuasive writing:

> The most advanced secondary textbooks for English do not teach students to think critically or to write argument. Rather, they opt for vague discussions of 'persuasive writing.' One significant text of over 1,100 pages [claims] 'In a persuasive essay, you can select the most favorable evidence, appeal to emotions, and use style to persuade your readers. Your single purpose is to be convincing' [305]. The same might be said of propaganda and advertising. Argument, on the other hand, is mainly about logical appeals and involves claims, evidence, warrants, backing, and rebuttals...[10]

The cumulative assignments we discuss below are designed to develop independent facility in argumentation. In write-to-learn activities, students can collaborate in the process of generating ideas. In cumulative writing they may share drafts and support each other's articulation of ideas, but they are required to develop an independent voice and produce arguments.

We promote the idea of building blocks, adapting the assessment terminology of W. James Popham: writing assignments that progress and build on skill sets from close reading to complex argument.[11] Students should not be asked to produce argument-based written work without being taught the components of that logical structure. Notice, gentle reader, that we are not talking about *form* (beware the 'rules' of the five-paragraph paper, three-points of support, every paragraph beginning with a Main Idea and

---

[10] Hillocks, 'Forward', xvii.
[11] Popham, *Transformative Assessment in Action: An Inside Look at Applying the Process*, 27.

conclusions that re-state the thesis). Logic is more difficult than formula, and complex texts require complex arguments that cannot be boiled down to formulas. In the writing assignments that follow, students will move from answering questions to generating them. It is important to recognize that the assignments below are intentionally sequential.

Building block 1: Writing a close reading of a specific passage

In the course of the Shakespeare unit, the class has been collectively performing close readings of speeches and scenes. This first building block requires students to perform close readings independently, but with significant teacher scaffolding. The following example of a cumulative writing prompt asks students to consider Cassius's description of Caesar as a Colossus (1.2.134–60). In two paragraphs, the students will delineate how Cassius attempts to persuade Brutus to join the conspirators by enumerating and describing the moves in Cassius's persuasive strategy, and identifying the governing metaphor (the physical/material details Cassius employs).

This assignment does not ask students to develop an argument about 'why' Cassius says what he does – students get tripped up by making grand sweeping statements or definitive equations (Cassius = tempter; Brutus = dupe). Instead this assignment asks students to read closely into the 'how' of Shakespeare's language. Students need to be able to translate their attention to the details of their close readings into clear and coherent written work before we ask them to explain the 'why,' make complex arguments and analyse a text.

In an ideal classroom, this assignment would be repeated with another rich bit of text. The more students are asked to translate their close reading into compelling prose, the better.

Building block 2: Answering a narrow question

The next building block assumes that students are able to write close readings (building block 1). Now they will be asked to answer a question provided by the teacher, but the question should be extremely focused so that it demands a text-based argument in response.

For instance, the cumulative writing prompt should focus students on the murder of Caesar in 3.1. Brutus says, 'Stoop, Romans, stoop, / And let us bathe our hands in Caesar's blood / Up to the elbows and besmear our swords' (3.1.105–7). Look closely at the entire scene and answer why the conspirators 'Stoop, then, and wash' (3.1.111). In roughly two pages, use evidence from the text (close readings required) to argue why they willingly mark themselves in this fashion.

Teachers who are emphasizing the early modern historical context might extend this assignment by offering students historical readings related to the use of blood in early modern executions. It was not only popular to attend executions but also a common practice to dip one's handkerchief in the blood of the executed (beheaded, disembowelled, drawn and quartered, etc.). The blood was called mummia or mummy.[12] Students would incorporate this historical information into their analysis of Brutus's directions to the conspirators.

Building block 3: Answering a broader question

The virtue of the cumulative writing assignment in building block 2 is its focus, but students also need to be able to trace and argue points within the play as a whole. Although this cumulative writing assignment requires students to answer a question provided by the teacher, the question is broader in scope. A broader question requires students to choose evidence from across a specific Shakespeare text (not just in one speech or scene).

For instance, the cumulative writing prompt for building block 3 should ask students to consider the reason for the animals included in *Julius Caesar*. Pre-writing activities: list the animals mentioned and/or described in the play. Categorize the animals: ask yourself where they are mentioned, by whom and what they are doing? In roughly three pages, use evidence from the text (close readings required) to argue *why* the animals are included at all. A well-crafted argument not only collates supporting evidence but also accounts for divergent evidence.

Teachers who are emphasizing critical lenses might extend this assignment by offering students one or two examples of eco-criticism. Scholars doing this work investigate human–animal interactions and many research the changing patterns of these interactions over time (e.g. the role of pets in different historical moments).[13] Students would incorporate this literary scholarship into their analysis of animals in *Julius Caesar*.

Building block 4: Student-generated questions

Advanced learners become independent thinkers and writers and gain facility with complex texts through learning to ask and answer good questions. A good question for an advanced learner to ask is neither too small nor plot driven: asking why the Ides of March are dangerous for

---

[12] Noble, 'The Fille Vierge as Pharmakon: The Therapeutic Value of Desdemona's Corpse'.
[13] Shannon, *The Accommodated Animal: Cosmopolity in Shakespearean Locales*.

Caesar cannot be answered by a student's argumentative essay. A good question is one that is not too large: asking how the assassination of Caesar affects the Roman Empire cannot be answered in five to six pages, no matter how good the argumentation. Part of building block 4 requires students to choose an appropriate topic that can be answered in an effective manner.

For instance, the cumulative writing prompt for building block 4 should ask students to devise a question that interests them and that can be answered using support from the text (close reading required). Pre-writing activities: choose an appropriate topic, focus on a small amount of text, ask questions about the details you notice and ask yourself how these are related to the play as a whole. In five to six well-crafted pages, create an argument based on your reading of the specific topic and excerpts. Explain and unpack the significance of those passages for your reader and argue their significance within the larger context of the play. You must explain why your argument matters and how it will help others to understand the text.

Typical major projects

If advanced learners work throughout a Shakespeare unit completing write-to-learn activities and the building block cumulative writing assignments, those pages of process, response and critical analysis should be sufficient demonstration of facility with complex texts. Some curricula will close a Shakespeare unit with a major project. Below we address the pros and cons of creative and critical writing projects.

Typical major project 1: Random acts of research

It is common practice to assign a research paper to advanced learners in a Shakespeare unit. In the US, Advanced Placement classes frequently expect students to produce an independent analysis of a play supported by research of literary scholarship. What is the purpose of such a research paper? There are certainly skills required to narrow topics and find appropriate sources, and students can develop their thinking as they pursue a topic deeply and learn to record or catalogue their findings. Research on a particular Shakespeare play often brings students to scholarly databases, perhaps under the guidance of a librarian who opens up vast resources.

A teacher may expand students' thinking about a play by providing close readings of a particular critical text. It is true that literary criticism provides excellent examples of complex texts, but it is written for a specific audience of specialists who are engaged in a rich scholarly dialogue that occurs across centuries. We encourage teachers to think about what students are capable of doing with these resources. After all, Shakespeare scholarship dates back to the late seventeenth century. Is it reasonable to expect advanced learners to be able to distinguish the scholarly trends of different eras (Samuel Johnson, Orson Welles and Nelson Mandela have all commented on *Julius Caesar*)? Entering into this dialogue requires expertise that is attained through graduate studies. When a writing assignment requires advanced learners to incorporate literary scholarship, many are unable to perform sophisticated close readings of literary scholarship, even when their close readings of a Shakespeare play are complex, original and thought provoking. Is the purpose of assigning a research project within a Shakespeare unit to create a mini-scholar/expert? If not, what is the goal?

The problem might be clearer if we provide an example in a different discipline. Imagine an introductory biology class studying vital organs in mammals. Now imagine an assignment that requires students to find articles in the *New England Journal of Medicine*, *JAMA* and *Lancet* in support of a paper on liver functions. This would seem a ludicrous assignment because even the most advanced learners do not have access to the language employed by specialists, whether they are medical researchers or Shakespeare scholars. It is useful for students to discover that there is a rich scholarly dialogue about the plays and material culture, production history, literary criticism, historical contexts, etc. But this is different from the hunt-and-gather methods of random acts of research. Purpose, purpose, purpose.

Typical major project 2: Creative writing

It is also common to assign a final creative project to culminate a Shakespeare unit. These assignments can be valuable when students are engaged on a personal, emotional and creative level. For instance, advanced learners can be empowered when they are offered an opportunity to rewrite an ending, change a genre or alter a character's fate. The best of these assignments require advanced learners to independently synthesize close readings, analyses and arguments. With that foundation, creative work can be astonishing and a clear demonstration of their facility with complex texts.

Unfortunately, many creative assignments are actually write-to-learn assignments disguised as Major Projects. Many are intended as 'rewards' for students at the end of a unit, inviting students to make Shakespeare their own – modernizing settings, language and 'themes' – without providing a structure that takes advantage of the analytical work they have been doing throughout the unit. The difference is between asking students to write a Facebook page for Cinna the Poet ('going out now to see the bros about the rebellion') and asking them to create a script that sets Cinna and the Plebeians in, for instance, Tiananmen Square. Earlier we noted that write-to-learn exercises give students the skills to modernize or reset a scene, including the close attention to textual detail that close reading enables. We also noted that these kinds of details are required for interpretive and performative opportunities such as creative Major Projects.

We are aware of, and admire, works of art that adapt, appropriate and spin-off Shakespeare's plays. The purpose in our classrooms, however, is to encourage creativity of expression without requiring genius (this book is not intended for creative writing classrooms: that is another book). The purpose of a creative major project should be to demonstrate facility with complex texts: these assignments can be extremely rewarding and fun, but that is not the ultimate purpose. When doing creative major projects, advanced learners need to be prompted to think analytically about the text at hand, and carefully about the changes they want to make. If teachers lose sight of the ultimate purpose, they risk having to assess creative major projects for effort, cleverness or entertainment value.

This chapter is artificially constrained by the topic of writing, and advanced learners may be interested in creative major projects that are performance based and include multimodal expression (digital, visual and musical). These, too, can be based on close analytical work and in the following chapter we discuss ways that rubrics can guide advanced learners to sophisticated performances of their knowledge.

Concluding thoughts

Composition pedagogy offers many strategies for the study of Shakespeare's plays to develop sophisticated written expression. Although the writing process privileges student choice and the development of student voice, this chapter demonstrates the importance of promoting and cultivating purpose when creating writing assignments for advanced learners. As we have argued throughout this book, the true benefit of studying Shakespeare's work is to develop facility with complex texts. Writing assignments should be equally purposeful. Whether the assignment is formative or cumulative, the goal is to develop more sophisticated written expression through assignments that require students to move from explication, annotation and rehearsal to analysis, synthesis and argumentation.

7

Assessment with purpose

We have offered multiple ways to guide students through Shakespeare's plays, and we have emphasized throughout that the purpose of teaching Shakespeare is for students to gain facility with complex texts. In this chapter we discuss ways to assess whether students are making progress toward that facility. It should not surprise you, gentle reader, that we will hammer on *purpose* as we articulate strategies for formative and summative assessments. For this chapter especially we want to emphasize that assignments should not be given, and assessments should not be used, unless there is a purposeful reason for doing so. At the same time, we recognize that assessment purposes are not completely within the control of the individual instructor, particularly as students are preparing for university-level work. As we discussed in Chapter 1 (purpose), our belief is that Shakespeare's plays should be *taught* because they are complex texts of the highest order and students need to acquire the intellectual habits and strategies that enable them to engage with such texts independently.

Our thinking is aligned with those who create state and national assessments in the UK and the US: we are all concerned with having students demonstrate facility with complex texts. Unfortunately the pressures for performance on specific examinations can skew teaching practices and, worse, can confuse students about what is valuable and important about being able to make sense of a Shakespeare play. At the end of this chapter we will discuss the kinds of timed or 'on-demand' writing assessments that are required of many of our students, and how the focus on purpose in this book will serve these students well.

Although the chapter on writing assignments comes before this chapter on assessment, all assignments (written tasks, performances and creative work) should in fact *begin* with assessment: a careful consideration of what information an assessment will provide to the teacher and to the student. Whether a literature course is focused on Shakespeare's plays or includes the study of only one, there are key questions to ask in order to gauge the progress of your advanced learners during a given Shakespeare unit.

- What tasks will inform me about whether my students are progressing in their facility with this Shakespeare text?

- What evidence will a particular task (an assignment of written analysis, of a performance or of creative work) give me about the degree or quality of my students' independent facility with Shakespeare?

- How do I know when my students will be able to formulate their own questions and answers about a Shakespeare text?

- How will I know if and when my students are ready to transfer their skills to unfamiliar Shakespeare texts and other complex texts?

In this chapter we provide a series of possibilities for assessing student progress. While we periodically reference *A Midsummer Night's Dream* to provide a textual example, these assessment strategies are designed to be transferable to a unit on any Shakespeare play. We begin with a discussion of the use of rubrics to communicate the *purpose* of assignments – written analysis, performances and creative work – to students. We offer strategies for formative or process assessments that provide information for teachers as they plan and carry out units and to students as they make progress toward unit goals. Drawing on our 'building block' writing assignments in Chapter 6, we suggest rubrics that can assess these assignments, particularly as advanced learners become more independent. Finally, we review the kinds of summative assignments teachers often use to complete a Shakespeare unit: the research paper, creative work and timed or on-demand essays. We are not convinced that a rich Shakespeare unit really needs a final assessment, but we understand why teachers may choose to administer one to give students practice with demanding written and examination forms.

Rubrics

Whatever the assessment tool used, our consistent goal is for student work to present a clear, coherent and compelling argument about a text. We expect an argument to be supported by appropriate evidence arising from close reading: evidence that is selected and presented with care rather than offered up as a string of quotations. We have each spent our academic careers agonizing over how to elicit this kind of work from students, especially in response to complex texts. We know from experience how difficult it is to improve student writing, and we recognize that one size will not fit all.

US teachers use *rubrics* to describe how student work will be assessed; in the UK, the word *rubric* describes the instructions for creating a document, such as an examination paper. For this book, a rubric is a teacher-created (not generic) grid or table that outlines specific dimensions of a given assignment and the quality of student work that is expected for each component. We offer some general categories and ideas for rubrics in this chapter because teachers who utilize rubrics for the assessment of student writing, performance and creative work gain an organizational tool for thinking carefully through their expectations. Through assigning points (or marks, or a numeric value) to different levels of accomplishment ('exemplary–developing–insufficient', for instance), a rubric can also communicate the relative value of different components of the assignment.

Thus, in combination with an assignment prompt, a rubric provides a purposeful delineation of an assignment that can demystify the expectations and make its assessment explicit and transparent. In addition, students become more independent as advanced learners as they utilize a rubric to self-assess. Used well, a rubric can (as James Popham describes) distinguish wretched from rapturous work in a transformative way.[1] With the help of a teacher's well-crafted rubric, advanced learners can recognize how to adjust their tactics and become more successful as well as independent.

For a Shakespeare unit, the most useful rubric is one created by a teacher for a specific assignment. Here are rather standard categories for assessing writing, performance and creative work that we find useful:

- Focus
- Supporting detail
- Organization
- Fluency
- Conventions

As our 'building block' writing assignments suggest, there can be a sequence for assignments where scaffolding (of teacher inputs and direction) is systematically removed and student production becomes more independent. But a rubric should describe expectations of quality in student work in ways that capture more than a progression in independence. Table 1, Expectations for the quality of student work, shows some examples in categories that can help explain to students the *quality* expected in their work.

Not every assignment requires an individual rubric, but we use rubrics here to emphasize that complex texts written, performed and created in response to Shakespeare deserve a considered, rather than formulaic, response. As Tom Romano writes, every act of evaluation or feedback on student work should be purposeful and 'calculated to induce the student to

---

[1] Popham, *Transformative Assessment*, 90.

Table 1 Expectations for the quality of student work

Quality	Written work	Performance-based work	Creative work
Focus	The quality of a written assignment's focus is determined by its thesis and how effectively an interpretive perspective is communicated. Placing a thesis statement at the top of an essay is one thing; addressing and developing it throughout is a more sophisticated expression of focus.	The quality of a performance-based assignment's focus is determined by its organizing principle and how effectively that interpretive perspective is communicated. In a student performance, focus means a shared and consistent interpretive perspective on characterization, setting, costuming and overall direction.	The quality of a creative assignment's focus is determined by its organizing principle and how effectively that point of view is communicated. In creative work, focus is often demonstrated by control, subtlety and precision.
Supporting detail	The quality of a written assignment's supporting detail is determined by the selection, presentation and employment of sources from within or outside the text. The use of sources in an essay is one thing; the use of sources in an integrated fashion is a more sophisticated employment of supporting details.	The quality of a performance-based assignment's supporting detail is determined by the selection and presentation of characterization, setting, costuming and overall direction.	The quality of a creative assignment's supporting detail is determined by the multifaceted correspondence between the original Shakespearean work and the new work (both macro correspondences like themes, and micro correspondences like poetic rhetoric).

Quality	Written work	Performance-based work	Creative work
Organization	The quality of a written assignment's organization is determined by the relationships among the focus and the supporting details included. The structure of a written work should be determined by the task. The intentional placement of one argument before another, or one supporting detail before another, is an important element of organization.	The quality of a performance-based assignment's organization is determined by its coherence and the creation of a unified point of view.	The quality of a creative assignment's organization is determined by the relationships among the focus and the supporting details included. The structure of a creative work should be determined by the task.
Fluency	The quality of a written assignment's fluency is determined by its diction, concision, variety of sentence structure and the deployment of transitions as signposts for organization.	The quality of a performance-based assignment's fluency is determined by diction, gesture and blocking.	The quality of a creative assignment's fluency is determined by diction and poetic rhetoric.
Conventions	Punctuation, spelling, grammar and usage. (See textbox on Grammar)		

write again'.[2] Students need to have their efforts reinforced through assessments that focus on what they have created (the extent to which they meet the specifications of the assignment) and on the quality of their efforts. Useful rubrics offer precise academic language about where students need to direct their efforts in order to improve their facility with complex texts.

When we think about the student work that really excites us, those qualities are difficult to capture in a rubric. Should there be a category for originality? How would *A Midsummer Night's Dream* itself fair by this rubric as creative work? We know rubrics rarely describe the only categories of quality that matter. At the same time, a rubric can remind the teacher *not* to attempt to assess what she has not taught. In the assessment examples that follow, a rubric can help teachers explicate their expectations and organize their responses to student work.

Formative assessments

We offer strategies for formative assessment within a Shakespeare unit which are short assignments for the specific purpose of gauging student progress. These assessment activities make sense to supplement or supplant reading quizzes, for example. We recognize the urge to 'force' students to read by holding them accountable for independent reading, but we want to reiterate that such quizzing needs to be designed to forward the overall purpose: increased facility with complex text. If the goal of a quiz is simply to ensure basic character recognition or familiarity with the plot, it is unlikely that student success on the quiz is indicative of their ability to read closely on the level that a Shakespeare play requires.

We utilize brief writings to capture students' ideas and to encourage advanced learners to reflect on their learning, and suggest fast written assessments of student participation within active groups. In this way a Shakespeare unit for advanced learners can include multiple write-to-learn activities and formative assessments that can generate data about what students know, and can help an instructor gauge what other instruction or practice students need in order to increase their facility with complex texts. Formative assessment data should aid teachers as they organize, pace and revise their unit; formative assessments also give students evidence of their progress.

Assessing progress and reflecting on learning

If the goal of a *Midsummer Night's Dream* unit is to focus on women, and a particular classroom discussion has focused on female friendships

---

[2]Romano, *Clearing The Way: Working with Teenage Writers*, 109.

Alex Jennings as Oberon and Lindsay Duncan as Titania in Adrian Noble's 1996 film A Midsummer Night's Dream.

in the play, the teacher could ask students to write for ten minutes at the end of class about Titania's description of her friendship with the votaress (2.1.121–37). In the ten minutes of writing, students will reveal the extent to which they are following the class discussion and becoming comfortable with the poetic discourse of the play. Teachers can read the student work quickly, looking for specific examples. A student who unpacks the imagery of pregnancy and/or mortality would demonstrate a more sophisticated facility with the complex text than one who misses the friendship altogether.

It is also appropriate to use a formative assessment to gather student reflections on a unit as it progresses, tapping into the connections advanced learners are making between the close readings of the text and our twenty-first-century world. If a previous class session has analysed three images from productions of *Dream* for depictions of Athens and the forest, the start of the next class might include a 'warm-up' or beginning activity that asks pairs or small groups of students to discuss which setting of the play seems more like the one they live in, and why. Teachers can listen for instances in which students articulate a detailed understanding of the setting they have chosen, pressing as necessary for the kinds of supporting detail that enable advanced learners to construct an argument (e.g. their understanding of the fairy and the human kingdoms of the play).

As noted in the textbox on 'Managing formative assessments', if teachers design a class session to move fluidly from student writing to discussion to participation in small groups – sometimes with students under direct instruction, and at other times with them directing their own learning – there will be multiple opportunities to assess progress. Not all of the assessment needs to be provided by a teacher; instead, she can oversee an exchange of productive feedback. Advanced learners are capable of reading and commenting on each other's work. This work may be an informal paragraph or list meant to capture ideas as they are generated; it may be a tableau created to illustrate the power relations in a given scene (e.g. 1.1 of *Midsummer*); it may be a response to how another student intends to update the flower/drug that enables Titania to be enamoured with the ass-headed Bottom. In any case, in a classroom where student-to-student conversations matter, increasingly independent analysis can thrive.

Managing formative assessments

Here is a radical principle for a successful Shakespeare unit: at the end of each day, the students should be exhausted and the teacher should be energized. Information from assessments can provide important guidance to the instructor and to the student, but that does not mean that every assessment requires extensive feedback. Students may need to be weaned from such dependence: a point or a grade should not be everything they need to know about their progress relative to the overall course goals. We have known teachers try to measure and mark every move each student makes, and while their intentions and efforts are laudable, the impact of all these assessments is likely not as great as the energy required.

Some student work needs only collection because its value is in the learning that arises during the activity, not from any immediate product. For instance, if students write an 'exit slip' at the end of class to report on their new thinking about Hippolyta because of an extended discussion comparing her to Titania, a teacher *may* want to collect these writings as one way to gauge the students' understanding. But it may be enough to have students capture these new ideas for *their* future use, and the exit slip can be incorporated into an ongoing writing or response journal.

Such a journal (or folder or other writing-collection device, digital or on paper) need not become a mountain of text for the teacher to process. A teacher should establish a routine for how students can collect their ideas that arise from writing-to-learn activities, such as listing, silent discussions, free writes, exit slips, and more. These writings can be part of class or an aspect of work for home. A key component of a regular writing routine is then labelling the work – establishing a naming convention, in the language of programming – that allows easy access to it. A Shakespeare unit can then identify perhaps three times in the calendar where a lottery determines what part of the collected work is assessed. A teacher can draw from a hat (literally) the assignments that will be marked or recorded as complete. Such a random drawing might have the enthusiastic teacher of Shakespeare waxing on about the vagaries of fate, but the lottery demonstrates clearly to the students that the written work of the class is intended for *their* benefit as learners. Typically the first random drawing will result in students who claim (loudly) that the only work they did *not* complete were the assignments that were chosen. Soft-hearted teachers may wish to include a 'free choice' option.

For much informal writing and practice, general feedback, along the lines of 'good work' and 'nice job' or '✓+', communicates a basic level of completion. Specifically *academic* feedback is more valuable and should be deployed constantly in discussion and carefully on student written work. Academic feedback is useful to students: it helps them understand where more effort and attention will get them positive results.[3] It is the difference between nodding an affirmation at a student who speaks and repeating or rephrasing a key idea so that students know *what* is good about what has been offered. In written work, academic feedback points the student to the criterion (as, for instance, established by the rubric) and helps him or her understand what aspect of a required component may be excellent or missing.

It is worth considering how new digital tools and the ubiquitous mobile phone may also allow teachers to assess student progress in a Shakespeare unit. Using web-based programs such as Poll Everywhere (http://polleverywhere.com) that utilizes SMS messaging, or TurningPoint (http://turningtechnologies.com), which is a PowerPoint add-on that requires 'responseware' (e.g. clickers), teachers can create participation polls that almost instantly gauge and report student responses anonymously. Whereas some teachers use such devices to determine simple student content knowledge, and others use games in the hope of motivating student engagement (please do not ask us about the game in which Shakespeare is the goalkeeper), it is possible to elicit more intriguing and generative ideas through these tools. A class could be best served by giving the creation of polls over to the students, who might poll their classmates to test out claims and arguments about characters, speeches and/or scenes.

Assessing participation and individual contributions to a group

Teachers who are incorporating theatre-based practices into their Shakespeare unit need to think about assessing informal participation in ways that

---

[3]Hattie, *Visible Learning for Teachers: Maximizing Impact on Learning*, 173.

emphasize that the dramatic exercises offer valuable insights into complex texts. A gifted facilitator – in our experience, theatre company education outreach specialists – may 'freeze' students in the midst of their theatrical experiments and elicit thoughtful and focused responses. There can be rich analysis when groups listen to each other and describe the decisions they made in blocking scenes or depicting characters based on a given text. But one instructor managing a large class in a less than ideal space may need to depend more on informal student writing to get to such critical and creative thinking. For instance, if students are enacting the rage, jealousy and antic confusions of Demetrius, Lysander, Hermia and Helena in 3.2, they likely will need a few minutes to take stock of their discoveries. Using a technique of *silent conversation*, a teacher could ask students to pass a single sheet of paper between pairs or in small groups. The prompt might ask students to discuss: why does Helena believe there is a conspiracy against her? Each student contributes examples of what has been said by the other characters.

More direct assessments of participation can be made through student self-report. At the most basic level, advanced learners might be asked to grade themselves at the end of a class session. An activity that could yield more useful data would ask students to identify three aspects of a particular characterization (e.g. a performance-based interpretation of Bottom in 3.1) that they intend to build on in the next active session, or details they would potentially incorporate as they consider that character in the next building block writing assignment. If such student processing of an activity is done in writing, a teacher will have information that reveals the progress students are making in their understanding of a scene. Even if the assessment an instructor makes is of the progress of the class as a whole, the act of assessment – of asking questions about process – emphasizes to the students that the group work matters, and that the teacher expects to inventory the student learning that results from theatre-based practices.

Grammar

Writing to future teachers in the UK, Mark Pike notes the impact of the National Curriculum and its requirement that literature teachers must increasingly also know English syntax and 'the meta-language of English'.[4] In the US, Harry Noden cautions that 'Discussing grammar in the teachers' lounge is still like stepping between two opposing 350-pound NFL linemen ... When the topic is grammar, teachers can become

---

[4]Pike, *Teaching Secondary English*, 53.

combative.'[5] Noden attempts to get teachers out of that combative stance by emphasizing that advanced learners benefit from thinking of the writer as an artist whose grammatical choices represent different brush strokes made to different effects. We too want to help teachers escape overly technical or even combative positions with regards to assessing grammar. The real question on both sides of the Atlantic in assessing a student's use of grammar is how much is helpful? Will marking every comma splice make Jane realize her grammatical mistakes and how to avoid them in the future? There is, of course, a spectrum between correcting typos and reformulating/rewriting sentences and ideas. While we believe that teachers should never edit their students' written work unless they have been explicitly asked to do so, we recognize the necessity of communicating to advanced learners that they will be judged on everything from the correctness of their grammar to the ideas they are working to express. Ideally, teachers should help students 'visualize the canvas of the entire piece of writing' while enabling advanced learners to pay careful attention to each sentence (punctuation, spelling, grammar and usage) and its contribution to the whole (focus, supporting details and organization).

Assessing building blocks

While we caution teachers against a generic rubric for assessing specific assignments, it can be helpful to use a consistent rubric as students work through the building block writing assignments detailed in Chapter 6.

Building block 1: Writing a close reading of a specific passage
Building block 2: Answering a narrow question
Building block 3: Answering a broader question
Building block 4: Student-generated questions

As we noted, it is helpful to think about creating a sequence of written assignments that asks students to be progressively more independent in their analysis of complex texts. Such a sequence is what James Popham calls a *Learning Progression*, 'a sequenced set of sub-skills and bodies of knowledge it is believed students must master en route to mastering a more remote curricular aim'[6]. While we do not believe that facility with complex texts is such a remote aim, we appreciate Popham's reminder that

---

[5]Noden, *Image Grammar, Second Edition: Teaching Grammar as Part of the Writing Process*, xiii.
[6]Popham, *Transformative Assessment*, 47.

assessments should focus on the most essential tasks within a sequence of learning activities. In other words, we must be very purposeful in how we describe our expectations for what students must do and intentional in how we scaffold their efforts. If they are struggling, we can recognize their difficulties and offer additional guidance and practice. Below, in Table 2, Expectations for building block writing assignments, we provide a guide, a blueprint for building rubrics that communicate expectations and allow students to recognize their own progress through the building blocks. The learning progression in the building blocks sequence is articulated here in terms of the most essential tasks for each writing assignment. We assume that the individual instructor will know the specific information to emphasize within each category, based on the level of skills of her students.

Table 2 Expectations for building block writing assignments

Quality	BB 1	BB 2	BB 3	BB 4
Focus	Given ten to twenty lines, advanced learners must delineate in a clearly articulated thesis HOW the Shakespearean text works rhetorically and poetically.	Given a specific Shakespearean scene or act, advanced learners must devise and articulate an answer to a teacher's prompt.	Given a broader question about a specific Shakespearean play, advanced learners must devise and articulate an answer to a teacher's prompt.	Given a Shakespearean play, advanced learners must devise and articulate an answer to their own original question.
Supporting detail	Advanced learners must select three to four words or phrases from the assigned text that best illustrate the focus they have chosen.	Advanced learners must select and present words, phrases and statements that best illustrate the answer they have devised.	Advanced learners must select, present and integrate words, phrases and statements that best illustrate the answer they have devised.	Advanced learners must select, present and integrate words, phrases and statements that best illustrate the original question they have chosen to answer.
Organization	Two paragraphs is an appropriate structure for this assignment because it is aimed to encourage advanced learners' attention to detail and discourage their use of rhetorical and argumentative filler. Paragraphs are presumed to include a topic or focusing sentence, multiple sentences of support and a conclusion and/or transition to the next ideas.	Three to five paragraphs is an appropriate length for this assignment because it encourages advanced learners to answer a narrow question and to determine the logical order for presenting the supporting details.	Multiple paragraphs supporting two or three key ideas is an appropriate length for this assignment because it encourages advanced learners to answer a broader question, determine the logical order for presenting the supporting details and signpost their argumentative moves.	Multiple paragraphs supporting each key idea is an appropriate length for this assignment because it encourages advanced learners to answer their own original question, determine the logical order for presenting the supporting details and signpost their argumentative moves.

Summative assessments

Assessing research

A good rubric will help an instructor avoid what we described in Chapter 6 as 'random acts of research' by communicating to the student how to reference and use historical, literary and/or performance scholarship effectively. As we have noted, it is useful for students to discover that there is a rich scholarly dialogue about the plays and material culture, production history, literary criticism, historical contexts, etc. Emphasizing the value of student organization and fluency (by using the rubric below) should encourage advanced learners to demonstrate what they have found through research without losing their individual voice or becoming mired in the technical language of scholarship.

Students who know that they are expected to devise their own original research question will likely need to see models of good research questions, larger contextual questions that arise from the text but cannot be answered by only references to the text. By highlighting *original* in this rubric, we want to encourage students to claim a topic that matters to them, that

Table 3 Expectations for researched writing

Focus	Given a Shakespearean play or set of plays, advanced learners must devise and articulate an answer to their own original research question.
Supporting detail	Advanced learners must select, present and integrate words, phrases and statements from the Shakespearean play or set of plays that best illustrate the original research question they have chosen to answer. In addition, they must locate, select (e.g. verify the credibility of sources) and integrate scholarship related to their original research question. (NB: by asking advanced learners to incorporate scholarship into their written assignments, teachers should be asking them to perform close readings of those materials as well.)
Organization	Advanced learners must answer their own original research question by determining a logical order for presenting the supporting details (including scholarship) and signposting their argumentative moves.
Fluency	Advanced learners must integrate the technical discourse of their external sources and maintain their own unique voice, keeping an eye toward diction, concision, variety of sentence structure and the deployment of transitions as signposts for organization.

explores gaps they recognize in what they understand to be true in contemporary times and what was true for other Shakespeare audiences. They may wish to explore topics that arise from their identity (race, gender, socio-economic status) and the degree to which they see, or do not see, themselves reflected in the text they have studied. Their research might lead them to compare cultural norms, such as about the education of women, juxtapose reports of performance practices or follow intriguing leads to understand the relationships between love potions and poisoning.

Assessing summative performance-based work

Many teachers conclude a Shakespeare unit with a creative group performance that includes planning, directing, performing and often recording one or more scenes. Creative work by definition means making something new, and yet when teachers assign performance-based work the assessment they use should reinforce that they are paying close attention to what students understand about the *old*, the Shakespeare text itself. Teachers vary in the kinds of mise en scène adaptations they allow, and the extent to which the assigned scene is edited or translated. In keeping with the purpose of building facility with complex text, the assignment and assessment should make clear to the students that they will be evaluated on their ability to be attentive to the details. Therefore, both the assignment and the assessment should require that students have a deeply considered knowledge base prior to the creative summative assignment (e.g. going through the formative and building block assignments described in Chapter 6).

Because we focus on English literature teachers in this book (i.e. not drama teachers necessarily), we argue that the use of theatre-based practices is not really for an audience's pleasure; typically the English literature teacher is not 'teaching acting' or assessing students on their acting abilities. Teachers need to find ways to encourage and commend artistry and cleverness, but not assess students on what they have not been taught. Similarly, a summative performance-based project should not be assessed on its 'entertainment value'.

Writing is essential to a summative performance-based project, whether it is the adaptation of a scene or the thoughtful and intentional editing of lines for the performance script. Reflective writing is especially important when the work has been collaborative, but the teacher's goal should not be to referee who contributed what. Instead, students should be expected to write reflectively and, we think, extensively about their creative process, so that what is assessed is not the performance but the students' reflections on their learning from it: this can include their intentions, what they feel their production was able to achieve, what they were unable to achieve and what they would do differently in hindsight. In other words, the reflective essay offers advanced learners an opportunity to both justify and assess their creative process and product. Similarly a process or assignment that clearly values such reflection would be useful for the assessment of multimodal or multi-genre student work as a summative project. Table 4 is a blueprint for how to organize evaluations of summative performance-based projects.

Table 4 Expectations for creative performances and products

Focus	Given a Shakespearean play, advanced learners must devise and articulate the organizing principle for their original performance-based project. In the performance itself, focus means a shared and consistent interpretive perspective on characterization, setting, costuming and overall direction. In the reflective essay, advanced learners must articulate and assess which interpretive choices were effective/ineffective.
Supporting detail	Based on the chosen organizing principle for their original performance-based project, advanced learners must select and present specific unifying details with regards to characterization, setting, costuming and overall direction. In the reflective essay, advanced learners must articulate and assess which chosen details were effective/ineffective.
Organization	The quality of a performance-based assignment's organization is usually determined by its coherence and the creation of a unified point of view. In the reflective essay, advanced learners must articulate and assess which decisions about point of view were effective/ineffective.
Fluency	The quality of a performance-based assignment's fluency is usually determined by diction, gesture and blocking. In the reflective essay, advanced learners must articulate and assess which decisions about gesture and blocking were effective/ineffective.

The timed essay/on-demand writing

Some teachers conclude a Shakespeare unit by requiring students to demonstrate their facility with complex texts under pressure. Given a Shakespearean passage, scene, play or set of plays, and often unfamiliar material, such as from a play the class has not studied, advanced learners are required to devise and articulate an answer to a question, or create and support an argument within a limited amount of time (usually in one sitting). Such tasks are typically associated with preparing students for examinations that are external to the particular classroom or school (in the US, AP examinations or IB certification; in the UK, GSCE or A levels).

US students are likely to encounter Shakespeare questions on the Advanced Placement examination.[7] In the UK Shakespeare's plays are central in the tests of the National Curriculum. It is interesting to compare UK and US expectations for on-demand writing. US English language and literature teacher and consultant Jim Burke writes:

> We are quick to resist and even dismiss the writing-on-demand genre as a distraction, an intrusion, a discordant note in the otherwise elegant music we want our curriculum to make. We often regard this genre as inauthentic, useless, even meaningless. And yet, our students encounter this genre everywhere: on final exams, formative assessments, district and state assessments; not to mention college placement exams and those tests, such as the SAT, ACT, and Advanced Placement, that are central to the college-bound student's future success.[8]

It is the artificial constraints of on-demand writing that may frustrate the US teacher who is more pedagogically comfortable with writing process activities (drafting, feedback, revision, etc.). Preparation for on-demand writing tasks is likely to be understood in the US as 'test prep' rather than instruction. Students, after all, need specific skills in order to successfully parse out the requirements of the writing prompt, and they need to be able to organize their ideas swiftly. Instructors need to prepare students for this kind of task by alerting students to the scoring criteria and helping them imagine their anonymous readers.

In contrast, the UK examination process seems to take test preparation in its stride, as unabashedly central to instruction. While accountability pressures and school ranking in league tables necessarily preoccupy some UK school leaders, there is a forthright and extensive investment in preparing students for particular examinations with teacher resources. As Peter Woolnough writes, 'As soon as the set sections for a given year are known, publishers, advisers, departmental colleagues and the QCA [Qualifications and Curriculum Authority] will be feverishly at work, producing guides, sample questions, annotated copies of the scenes, schemes of work and multimedia packages.'[9] Such rich resources can supplement a teacher's repertoire, but their existence alone does not eliminate the necessity of choosing well with a purpose in mind (for more examples of frames and topics for Shakespeare study, see Chapter 8).

Again, we want to emphasize the purposefulness of assessment, and it seems that on-demand writing is a legitimate way to determine whether advanced learners are becoming independent in their facility with complex texts. Teachers may want to use rubrics to assess time-constrained writing

---

[7]Metzger, 'Shakespeare for a New Age', 22.
[8]Burke, *The English Teacher's Companion*, 309.
[9]Woolnough, 'Catering for an Assessment-Driven Curriculum', 148.

in order to both streamline and focus their response to what students are able to produce. Adapting the 'building block' rubrics we offer above could be useful, especially in reminding students about the level and kinds of specific supporting detail that they are expected to muster in response to the prompt.

Teachers (especially in the US) may want to remind advanced learners that the purpose of on-demand writing assessment includes fairness, in that such tasks give every student an equal starting point.[10] Teachers may want to add a row to the rubric to include credit for the strategies for preparation that advanced learners should follow. The rubric should certainly include the individual instructor's expectations about the use of academic vocabulary, and the degree of emphasis on correctness, including the appropriateness of employing the first person ('I').

Once the students have completed their on-demand writings, the teacher assessment rubric can be a useful beginning for student reflection on performance. Advanced learners can use the descriptive categories to understand places where their close reading would have benefited from more precision, or their arguments needed more substantial support. Carol Jago recommends that teachers re-purpose the results of on-demand tasks as first drafts, perhaps as a surprise to students, but giving them reason to reconsider their ideas and revise their expression.[11]

Assessing advanced learners' writings about performance

While many literature teachers provide their advanced learners with the opportunity to write about performances (both live and on screens), it is important to remember that theatre, film and television writing are three distinct fields. Just as a biology teacher would not ask her students to write about what they see in a microscope's lens without first teaching them the broad strokes of how a microscope works and the language and the skills to decipher and interpret what they are seeing, so too English teachers should not ask our students to decipher and interpret performances without first teaching them the impact of the performance frame (e.g. television tends to eschew the wide shot) and the language to decipher and interpret what they are seeing (e.g. when alternating point of view shots are used in a film). This is all to say that the effective assessment of writing about performances can only occur if the teacher has given the advanced learners the tools to do the interpretive work.

---

[10] Burke, *The English Teacher's Companion*, 310.
[11] Jago, *Papers, Papers, Papers: An English Teacher's Survival Guide*, 58.

Table 5 Expectations for on-demand timed writing

Focus	Given a Shakespearean passage, scene, play or set of plays, and perhaps unfamiliar/new material, advanced learners must devise and articulate an answer to a question, or create and support an argument, within a limited amount of time (usually in one sitting).
Supporting detail	Advanced learners must select, present and integrate words, phrases and statements from the Shakespearean play or set of plays. They may have to draw on their memory to quote directly from a text.
Organization	Advanced learners must determine a logical order for presenting the supporting details and signposting of their argumentative moves.
Fluency	Advanced learners must maintain their own unique voice, keeping an eye toward diction, concision, variety of sentence structure and the deployment of transitions as signposts for organization.

Concluding thoughts

In a Shakespeare unit the purpose of assessment is to inform the instructor and the individual student about her progress toward facility with complex texts. A good assessment underlines what is valuable and important, and allows students to understand the quality of their performance. Ideally, a progression of assessments should enable students to move from responding to teacher-structured prompts to asking and answering questions of their own design. Ultimately, assessments help teachers to know whether students can utilize these facilities with new or unfamiliar complex texts. Purpose, purpose, purpose!

8

Applications

As a way of concluding, we offer a chapter that provides different applications of our approach to teaching Shakespeare to advanced learners. The applications are divided and organized according to the approaches we have discussed in each preceding chapter. These applications are not intended to comprise a unit of study; rather, they are meant to illustrate strategies that teachers can adapt as they work to increase their particular students' facility with complex texts. In other words, this chapter offers methods for teaching Shakespeare with a purpose, incorporating close reading, framing, informal learning communities, dynamic language study, dynamic history, active approaches and writing assignments. We have chosen *Macbeth* as the central text for the examples in this chapter, but these approaches are appropriate for any of Shakespeare's plays.

Framing

As we discuss in Chapter 2, the frame for a Shakespeare unit should guide the instructional design and suggest options for starting places and entry points to the play. Or, in the case of a classroom that uses targeted excerpts from multiple plays, the frame should organize how students consider *Macbeth* in juxtaposition with other Shakespeare plays. Furthermore, a frame is an interpretive lens that should be interrogated with the students, rather than something presented to them as the *only* lens for *the* correct interpretation or analysis. Frames should be generative instead of reductive.

One topic or frame for *Macbeth* is *substitution* and the question of equivalence. As many students will know, the title of the play, *Macbeth*, is traditionally substituted with a different moniker, *The Scottish Play*, whenever mentioned in a theatre. The play is thought to be so unlucky that the mere mention of its proper name will doom the cast and crew to unmentionable horrors. There is no other play – classical or modern – whose name must be substituted for another. Using the frame of *substitution*, students can investigate how the play, the play's history and/or the play's performance history are obsessed with or haunted by this topic. Such

Christophe Cagnolari, Nolan Kennedy and Leese Walker as the weird sisters in the Strike Anywhere Performance Ensemble's 2009 production of Macbeth Variations II. *Photograph by Fred Scott.*

a frame offers a good opportunity to provide a basic historical context for the first performances of the play: Queen Elizabeth I died childless, and the throne went to her cousin, the king of Scotland, King James. Historically, then, a king replaced a queen, a Scottish man replaced an English woman and the Stuart line replaced the Tudor line: these substitutions were not seamless nor invisible for the English subjects, who were being told for the first time that they were part of something larger than England, which King James coined 'Great Britain'. *Macbeth*, as a play, is clearly engaging with the early modern fascination with *substitution* and *equivalencies*: what can be substituted for something else without a significant difference or loss?

Within the frame of *substitution* the study of the play might begin at the beginning, with the opening scene. The witches begin by asking when they will meet again ('In thunder, lightning, or in rain?' (1.1.2)), and students may not immediately note that the witches both separate and make equivalent these various aspects of stormy weather. This type of substitution may not appear to be significant until students are asked to link it with other, more unequal, equivalencies: 'When the battle's lost and won' (1.1.4); and 'Fair is foul, and foul is fair' (1.1.11). Is there no difference between a battle that is won and a battle that is lost? Are there really no differences between the winners and losers? Likewise, what does it mean to assert that there are no differences between something fair and something foul? Is everything a potential substitution for everything else? What type of world view allows all things to be equivalent?

Another potential frame is *action*. What is the nature of action in the play? While it is customary to praise someone for being 'a person of action', *Macbeth* encourages its readers and audience members to ask if being a person of action is really a positive trait. This frame suggests another starting point, slightly later in the play when the witches return in 1.3. In this scene, one of the witches describes how she has been watching a sailor's wife 'munch' chestnuts. She narrates that when the woman refused to share the food with her, she hatches a revenge plot in which she will torment the unsuspecting sailor, proclaiming, 'I'll do, I'll do, and I'll do' (1.3.10). It is important to call the students' attention to the verb tense employed by the witch: the eternal present tense. By framing the discussion through *action*, teachers can enable their students to interrogate exactly what propels the three witches to work together. Is enacting revenge for unshared chestnuts an appropriate motive for action? And does one's assessment of motive impact one's view of action? Does the witches' continuous action – eternally 'doing' their revenge – impact the way we understand what it is, or what it takes, to commit oneself to action? When should action cease? Who is responsible for action or the need for inaction? And how does Macbeth's relationship with the witches impact the way we understand his desire for action?

A third frame for *Macbeth* is *desire*, and the guiding questions might ask: is Macbeth's desire ever sated? What will make him feel secure and satisfied with his acquisition of power? For this frame, an effective starting point is 3.2.4–37, in which Lady Macbeth begins by wondering why Macbeth is not content (after all, they successfully orchestrated the death of the king, and Macbeth's succession to the throne) and infamously asserts 'what's done is done' (3.2.12). Why is it not 'done' for Macbeth? Why does Macbeth describe his mind as being 'full of scorpions' (3.2.36)? What would it take for Macbeth to have a mind that is scorpion free? Is the scorpion external to Macbeth (if so, how did it get there?; who or what put it there?), or is there a way to think about Macbeth as the scorpion? It could be useful to combine the class's analysis of desire (sated or unsated) with an analysis of Lady Macbeth's desire (1.5.1–54). Lady Macbeth's reaction to the letter from Macbeth, in which he describes how the witches have prophesied his advancement, provides an excellent place to interrogate what she desires and what she is willing and capable of doing. Again, through the frame of *desire*, advanced learners will be able to think through the way the play divides the Macbeths.

Modelling close reading

We believe that every Shakespeare unit will require a teacher to model, perhaps multiple times, close readings of passages, speeches or scenes. As we have discussed in detail in earlier chapters, the modelling we imagine is parallel to how writing teachers demonstrate revision choices through a kind of out-loud close reading of their works-in-progress. Teaching Shakespeare requires such a demonstration, so that students can witness how a reader creates an interpretation of a speech or scene by selecting and parsing key words and phrases and then combining those details into a well-reasoned argument. The teacher must thoroughly prepare to offer a thoughtful interpretation/analysis of the passage and make it clear to her advanced learners that this is *one* reading, among many.

As we have noted, it is often very powerful when advanced learners have close readings modelled for them that contradict each other. For instance, there are radically different interpretations of Lady Macbeth's famous request to 'unsex me here' (1.5.41). While some read this line as a request to be made masculine, others read it as a request to cease being a reproductive (and, by extension, a loving) woman. Teachers who model close reading need to remind students that while not everyone will see/interpret/perform the text in the same way, not all perspectives are equally well argued and are therefore not equally valuable. Simply because there is ambiguity in the text does not mean that all readings are compelling (e.g. it would not be compelling to argue that 'unsex me here' means that Lady Macbeth is sexually unfulfilled).

Below is an example of a close reading of Macbeth's first soliloquy (1.3.130–42) read through the frame of *substitution*.

1 Read aloud (or have it read), perhaps more than once.

2 The frame of *substitution* establishes the questions to be asked of this soliloquy. Advanced learners often appreciate a teacher who demonstrates how focus on the particularity of the speech/dialogue/ bit of text can actually help limit their obligation to explain and explain and explain. Thus, the frame helps to delimit the immensity of the topics and ideas that *Macbeth* could be about.

3 The modelling reader asks aloud: what does Macbeth know about his desire to substitute himself for Duncan? It may be important to remind advanced learners that this is practically the first time we see Macbeth on stage (i.e. he does not appear until 1.3, after the second chanting of the witches). The reader asks: who is Macbeth?, and she can alert students to listen for what Macbeth is willing to say about himself. The reader wonders: what is his mental calculus for determining what he is or is not willing to do? And: why does he describe the discomfort of his own physical state when he is actually contemplating the murder of someone else?

4   Macbeth's use of the phrase 'supernatural soliciting' (130) offers
    an excellent place for the modelling reader to consult the OED:
    what exactly does *solicit* mean now, and is that different from early
    modern understandings of the word? If there is a Smartboard in
    the room, the teacher can turn to the dictionary entry and model
    how the word's changing meanings and usages provide additional
    perspectives on how Macbeth characterizes (and reacts to) the
    witches. To what extent is he suspicious of the witches as trying
    to 'incite, draw on, allure, by some specious representation or
    argument' (OED)? Out loud, as part of the modelling, the teacher
    can notice how *ill* and *good* are yoked together (131) and how the
    soliloquy ends with *being* and *nothingness* equated: 'And nothing
    is, but what is not' (142). Are these equivalencies similar to the
    witches' false equivalencies ('fair is foul, and foul is fair' (1.1.11))?
    What is the significance of Macbeth's willingness to yoke together
    these opposites? What happens if Macbeth's internal logic is similar
    to the witches' in this his first soliloquy?

5   Then a teacher can ask her advanced learners: does Macbeth
    make equivalent the truth of a fact with its goodness and virtue?
    A teacher can offer a translation of the sentence 'If ill, why hath
    it given me earnest of success, / Commencing in a truth' (132–3),
    unpacking the logical path that Macbeth follows. He is asking: if
    'the soliciting' is bad, why are the witches telling me something
    both good and true? It is Truth: I am Thane of Cawdor. If the
    'solicitation' is good, Macbeth wonders, 'Why do I yield to that
    suggestion' (134)?

6   Students need to interrogate whether the suggestion that Macbeth
    must kill to become king comes from the witches. Is the witches'
    prophecy that Macbeth will be 'King hereafter' (1.3.50) a prompt or
    directive for action? If not, from where does the suggestion come?
    The witches' prophecy sets Macbeth to 'horrible imaginings' (138).

7   It is important for the teacher (as modelling reader) to remind her
    advanced learners that Macbeth – the hero warrior – has just, in
    the previous scene, been described as cutting someone 'from the
    knave to th' chops' (1.2.22). Macbeth is clearly capable of an
    extraordinary level of bloodshed. Thus, the violence he is imagining
    does *not* seem out of character, and Macbeth is aware of this about
    himself. He is revealing his own agency ('My thought, whose
    murther yet is but fantastical' (139)) through his acknowledgement
    that his 'thought' is not merely a desire, but is instead a nascent
    plan of action.

8   In the end, students need to think through 'nothing is but what is
    not' (142). The question for the close reader to puzzle out is: what
    is 'nothing', and what is 'becoming something' for Macbeth.

It is often very effective to offer multiple close readings together, encouraging students to take ownership of the text by providing their own close readings. Another juicy bit in *Macbeth* occurs in 4.1.1–45, the witches' famous incantation over the cauldron. Modelling close reading within a frame of *desire* and/or *substitution*, the teacher can posit the guiding question as: who are these witches, and what do they want anyway? While many advanced learners will be familiar with portions of this scene, a framed discussion through the lens of *desire* and/or *substitution* will allow the students to consider what *and* who must be incorporated (literally ingested) in order to gain power.

The teacher who is modelling close reading can make a list of everything that goes into the cauldron: the various animals, poisoned entrails, specific animal parts, the liver of a Jew, the nose of a Turk, the lips of a Tartar, the finger of a prostitute's stillborn child, etc. In modelling close reading, the teacher may need to provide historical definitions for some of these ingredients, and this offers another effective moment to employ the OED. After cataloguing what the witches put into the cauldron, the teacher could ask: what does their 'cooking' tell us about the world of the witches, and whether or not they are themselves powerful? The genealogy of *soliciting* that we discussed above (1.3.130) is useful here as well: does the charm (the witches' brew) *solicit* power or agency? If so, from whom?

Ultimately, a modelled close reading through the frame of *desire* and/ or *substitution* should lead advanced learners to ask: why have the witches created this charm? What is the purpose of this scene? Are the witches really external to Macbeth or do they merely verbalize his deepest, usually unspoken, desires? Of course, there are no single or right answers to these questions. Advanced learners will have radically different readings of this scene, and the teacher's challenge is to demonstrate and then enable them to bring textual evidence to support their analyses.

It can be useful to point out to advanced learners the oversimplification offered in the notes to this passage. For instance, if the class is using the Arden edition of *Macbeth* (at the time of writing this book the most recent Arden edition is the second edition), the editor provides an oversimplified interpretation in which the parts of Jews, Turks, Tartars and stillborn children are included in the cauldron because they are 'unchristianed'. The editor seems to accept the witches' bizarre logic in which humans (dead or alive) and animals are equivalent. This is an editorial moment in which the editor fails to interrogate the witches' suspicious use of equivalencies. Should animal parts and human parts be viewed and treated as equivalent? What really links the ingredients together?

Dynamic language and informal learning communities

Today's advanced learners are accustomed to learning from each other in informal learning communities (see Chapter 1). The Porter scene in *Macbeth* (2.3.1–20) provides an excellent small amount of text to work through in an informal learning community because it offers so many interpretive choices. Students who already have some knowledge of the play might dismiss this scene as mere 'comic relief', and a concentrated group activity can push them to challenge any preconceived ideas they may have about the scene's significance. Potential guiding questions for an informal learning community are: what is the function of the Porter scene in *Macbeth*? Whether the small groups look at all of the following questions, or focus on ones they develop on their own, rich interpretive possibilities (beyond simple scene-changing humour) are likely to emerge. Informal learning communities can be structured to address topics such as:

1   Explore the history of the word 'equivocation' (in the OED) and connect the Porter's speech to the frame of *substitutions*. What is equivocation and what does it have to do with the rest of the play?

2   Explore the play's historical background, identifying and relating the context of the Gunpowder Plot with the plot of *Macbeth*. Annotated editions of *Macbeth*, like those by Arden, Oxford and Cambridge, usually provide this historical context in both the introductory materials and the textual glosses. What is the Gunpowder Plot and what does it have to do with the plot of *Macbeth*? And why does the Porter evoke this political context?

3   Locate images of *Macbeth* productions in order to think through how to costume the Porter. What do your costuming decisions reveal about your interpretations of the Porter?

4   Using a digital tool such as Animodo, 'direct' the Porter as an avatar, experimenting with how he should speak to the audience and/or himself. Pay particular attention to the line, 'I pray you, remember the Porter' (2.3.20–21). Who is he speaking to when he says this line, and what does this reveal about your interpretation of the character, scene and play?

5   Determine whether a production of *Macbeth* should utilize doubling for the character of the Porter (see the textbox on Doubling in Chapter 4). What other character(s) can the actor who plays the Porter play? If the actor playing the Porter is doubling roles, do you think the audience should be able to recognize the doubling? How might this decision impact your interpretation of the character?

The informal learning communities can work together to explore these questions and possibly create products to share with their classmates; or the questions can lead to a lively class discussion; or the questions could be treated as write-to-learn opportunities. The answers that the informal learning communities generate need not be enormous cumulative projects. Rather, they are designed to inspire the larger distributed knowledge of the class.

Theatre-based classroom techniques and explicit explorations of identity

As we stress in Chapter 4, there are many useful theatre-based classroom techniques for teaching Shakespeare's plays. Considering that one of the habits of learning valued by today's advanced learners is an explicit exploration of identity, we believe these theatre-based classroom techniques can be even more powerful, effective and impactful when they foster dialogues about identity. While there are many moments in *Macbeth* that when performed could enable these dialogues, we are particularly fond of the moment when Macduff travels to England to convince Malcolm that he should join the fight against Macbeth (4.3.44–137). An enigmatic scene in which Malcolm pretends to be a lustful, power-hungry tyrant to test whether Macduff is still loyal to Macbeth, 4.3 is often edited in productions so that the scene simply begins with Macduff learning of his family's murder (i.e. cutting out the discussion between Malcolm and Macduff). At the time of writing, there are no YouTube clips available of this scene, which suggests that it can offer unusual interpretive avenues because it is somewhat neglected.

Instructions for a theatre-based classroom technique that utilizes this scene should frame the activities in terms of identity. To begin, students should be asked to read the scene (4.3.44–137) independently (silently), and then they should be asked to read it chorally with one side of the room reading Malcolm's lines and the other side reading Macduff's. This can be repeated to establish the class's collective familiarity with the text, and then the class can be divided into groups of four to six students to perform interpretive readings of the scene. The students should be asked to consider:

1 How old is Malcolm, the future king of Scotland? Note that
   Malcolm is proclaimed King of Scotland at the very end of the play,
   and he has the last words of the play. How do interpretations differ
   if Malcolm is performed as being twelve years old versus thirty
   years old? How old is Macduff? Is there a large age gap between
   Malcolm and Macduff, or are they contemporaries? How should
   they be performed in terms of age? How do your answers to these
   performance questions affect and support your interpretation of this
   scene and the play?

2   Is Malcolm telling the truth when he claims that he is actually a virgin who has never told a lie (until now)? How should he be performed in terms of his veracity? How do your answers to these performance questions affect and support your interpretation of this scene and the play?

3   Why does Malcolm refer to Macbeth as 'black' (52) and 'Devilish' (117)? What does this rhetorical language signify about Malcolm's views of Macbeth? What happens when Macbeth is played by an actor of colour? How do your answers to these performance questions affect and support your interpretation of this scene and the play?

4   Macduff does not verbally protest Malcolm's vices (lechery and avarice) until Malcolm claims that he also loves chaos. How should Macduff react physically to each lie? Why does Macduff only verbally protest Malcolm's plans to 'confound / All unity on earth' (99–100)? How do your answers to these performance questions affect and support your interpretation of this scene and the play?

5   This scene is set in England. Should the location's change from Scotland be emphasized in any way? How and why? How do your answers to these performance questions affect and support your interpretation of this scene and the play?

As we noted in Chapter 4, theatre-based classroom techniques can be powerfully combined with write-to-learn activities so that advanced learners are made to reflect on their performance choices and to keep track of their growing understanding of characters and scenes.

Dynamic history 1 and informal learning communities

Another productive and effective topic that can be discussed and processed in informal learning communities is the authorship question, or the collaborative nature of Shakespeare's writing. Before university coursework students are rarely asked to consider what happens to their close readings of a Shakespeare play if Shakespeare is not the sole author of a given scene. While scholars widely acknowledge (and continue to research) Shakespeare's collaborations, this research rarely reaches advanced learners. For instance, since 1869 'the consensus of editorial and critical opinion' is that the printed version of *Macbeth* in the First Folio (1623) is the result of a collaboration between William Shakespeare and Thomas Middleton (1580–1627).[1] In particular, two of the witches' scenes (3.5 and 4.1), including the famous cauldron incantation, are thought to be collaborative

---

[1] Ewbank, 'The Tragedy of Macbeth: A Genetic Text', 1165.

endeavours between Shakespeare and Middleton. And yet this knowledge is frequently elided.

Inga-Stina Ewbank explains the popular resistance to acknowledging that The Bard wrote collaboratively:

> Twentieth-century distaste for the Hecate scenes is part of a more general purism, the theatrical equivalent of the scholarly search for authenticity, for the 'original' play. If *Macbeth* is seen as Shakespeare's play, with the stress on 'Shakespeare's' rather than on 'play,' then it is also natural to see Middleton's additions as contaminating a text 'owned' by Shakespeare. For all our knowledge of Renaissance stage practice, we find it easier to approach a play text in terms of the imaginative coherence imposed on it by an individual mind than as the record of stage performances.[2]

Ewbank goes on to note that despite the fact that knowledge of early modern performance conditions has become more widespread – 'We know that in the Elizabethan and Jacobean theatre the company, not the author, owned the text, and that in a play kept in active repertory cuts, revisions, and additions would be made to suit particular performances – at court, for example, or in the provinces – or to adapt the play to changing theatre conditions or popular taste'[3] – many in the twenty-first century cling to an outdated Romantic notion of the singularity of the author as genius, and Shakespeare as The Ultimate Author of Genius.

When this information is presented to advanced learners, it invites them to examine and question their own constructions of how Shakespeare worked as a playwright. At the level of the text, advanced learners should be asked to consider: does knowing that the witches are largely Middleton's contribution challenge, alter or affect their close reading of the scene? On a slightly broader level, advanced learners should be asked to consider: does the knowledge of Shakespeare's collaborative working conditions on *Macbeth* make the play less original? And on a meta-cognitive level, advanced learners should be asked to consider: are there issues of ownership for collaborative endeavours? Who 'owns' the work you just did with your classmates?

Dynamic history 2 and innovative performances of knowledge

As we note in Chapter 1, today's advanced learners also value assignments that allow them to present innovative performances of knowledge. The dynamism of history can be experienced in an activity that enables advanced learners to explore, discover and discuss why they think *Macbeth*

---

[2]Ewbank, 'The Tragedy of Macbeth: A Genetic Text', 1165.
[3]Ewbank, 'The Tragedy of Macbeth: A Genetic Text', 1165.

seems to invite historical/cultural substitution. One approach is to provide
the class with different historical documents that relate to *Macbeth* and ask
them (individually or in groups) to determine which historical contexts best
frame the study of *Macbeth*. This exercise challenges advanced learners to
think not only about how frames structure dialogues and interpretations
but also about how Shakespeare's plays are never fixed documents tethered
to one historical moment. This exercise might also challenge them to think
about which modes of communication are most effective for advanced
learners in the twenty-first century (e.g. print/handouts, short videos, audio
lectures/discussions, websites, etc.).

Below are historical documents related to *Macbeth*. Which document(s)
most effectively frame an introduction to the play, and what is the most
effective way to transmit this knowledge/frame to your peers?

1   Excerpt from Reginald Scott's *The Discoverie of Witchcraft* (1584)

The fables of Witchcraft have taken so fast hold and deepe root in
the heart of man, that fewe or none can (nowadays) with patience
indure the hand and correction of God. For if any adversitie,
greefe, sicknesse, losse of children, corne, cattell, or libertie happen
unto them; by & by they exclaime upon witches. As though
there were no God in Israel that ordereth all things according
to his will; punishing both just and unjust with greefs, plagues,
and afflictions in maner and forme as he thinketh good: but that
certeine old women here on earth, called witches, must needs be
the contrivers of all mens calamities, and as though they themselves
were innocents, and had deserved no such punishments. ... In like
manner I say, he that attributeth to a witch, such divine power, as
dulie and onelie apperteineth unto GOD (which all witchmongers
doo) is in hart a blasphemer, an idolater, and full of grosse impietie,
although he neither go nor send to hir for assistance.[4]

2   Excerpt from Raphael Holinshed's 'Chronicles of England, Scotland
and Ireland' (1587)

And sith it was a cause of suspicion of the mothers fidelitie toward
hir husband, to seeke a strange nurse for hir children (although hir
milke failed) each woman would take intollerable paines to bring
vp and nourish hir own children. They thought them furthermore
not to be kindlie fostered, except they were so well nourished after
their births with the milke of their brests, as they were before they
were borne with the bloud of their owne bellies, nay they feared least
they should degenerat and grow out of kind, except they gaue them
sucke themselues, and eschewed strange milke, therefore in labour
and painfulnesses they were equall, and neither sex regarded the heat

[4]Scot, *The Discoverie of Witchcraft*, 1, 7.

in summer or cold in winter ... In these daies also women of our countries were of no lesse courage than the men; for all stout maidens and wiues (if they were not with child) marched as well in the field as did the men, and so soone as the armie did set forward, they slue the first liuing creature that they found, in whose bloud they not onelie bathed their swords, but also tasted therof with the mouthes, with no lesse religion and assurance conceived, than if they had already been sure of some notable and fortunate victorie.[5]

3   Excerpt from King James' book *Daemonologie and News from Scotland* (1597)

The fearful abounding at this time, in this country, of these detestable slaves of the Devil, the witches or enchanters, has moved me (beloved reader) to dispatch in the post, this following treatise of mine, not in any way (as I protest) to serve for a show of my learning and ingenuity, but only (moved by conscience) to press thereby, so far as I can, to resolve the doubting hearts of many both that such assaults of Satan are most certainly practiced, and that the instruments thereof merit most severely to be punished, against the damnable opinions of two principally in our age. Whereof, the one called [Reginald] Scot, and Englishman, is not ashamed in public print to deny that there can be such a thing as witchcraft, and so maintains the old error of the Sadducees in denying spirits.[6]

4   Excerpt from Kim Sturgess's *Shakespeare and the American Nation* (2004)

So popular were [Shakespeare's] plays that on 10 May 1849, during a single evening, there were three separate audiences in the city watching *Macbeth* (something unlikely to occur today, despite a much larger metropolitan population) ... While prior to this night there had been a long-running trivial dispute between two actors about their respective performance style, it was popular hostility to the English that led to violence and bloodshed on a scale not seen before on the streets of New York. While the final statistics are still a matter of debate, it is thought that as many as thirty-one people died and 150 were injured following a truncated performance of *Macbeth* at the Astor Place Opera House by the British actor William Macready.[7]

5   Excerpt from Ayanna Thompson's 'What is a "Weyward" *Macbeth*?' (2010)

Macbeth often lures actors, directors, writers, and others into thinking that the 'Scottish play' does not carry 'the onerous burden of race.' This lure is so powerful ... that actors, directors, and

---

[5]Holinshed, 'Chronicles of England, Scotland and Ireland (1587)', 180–1.
[6]King James, *Daemonologie and News from Scotland*, 45.
[7]Sturgess, *Shakespeare and the American Nation*, 16, 41.

Ensemble from the Lafayette's 1936 production of Macbeth *(funded by the Federal Theatre Project) directed by Orson Welles. Library of Congress, Music Division, Federal Theatre Project Collection.*

writers often assume that they are the first to see the connections. *Macbeth* has long played a role in American constructions of race, from its appearance as the first Shakespearean play documented in the American colonies in 1699 (owned by the Virginia lawyer and plantation owner Captain Arthur Spicer) to a proposed Hollywood film version with an all-black cast. In the nineteenth century, *Macbeth* provided the context for the black actor Ira Aldridge's experimentation with whiteface performance as well as the classist-, racist-, and nationalist-based Astor Place Riot in 1849. Although Orson Welles's 1936 Federal Theatre Project version of *Macbeth* – commonly referred to as the 'Voodoo' *Macbeth* – is often discussed as the creation of Welles's singular and immense creative genius, there was an all-black FTP production the year before in Boston. Likewise, there have been numerous contemporary theatre companies that assume that they are unique in attempting to re-stage Welles's 'Voodoo' version. Moreover, there have been African-American, Asian-American, Native American (Alaskan and Hawai'ian), and Latino theatre companies that turn to *Macbeth* to help stage their own unique racial, ethnic, and cultural identities.[8]

---

[8]Thompson, 'What is a "Weyward" *Macbeth*?', 5–6.

It is important for advanced learners to consider what histories *Macbeth* has circulated in and through – comfortably and uncomfortably. As they consider interpretive choices, advanced learners can think about how a given historical moment might impact real or imagined performances. It is one thing for students to recognize the context of early modern history; it is another for them to be able to analyse a production in which other historical contexts are being invoked and employed (e.g. a Lady Macbeth who looks distinctly like Michelle Obama in dress, styling and race). Shakespeare's plays do not, and will not, stay adhered to one historical context in performance: that lack of stability requires advanced learners to hone their own interpretive skills and to recognize the interpretive moves made by others.

Cumulative writing assignments

As we discuss in Chapter 6, we promote argument-based writing while steering educators away from prescribing formulaic approaches that ape the conventions of literary criticism. Below we focus on the building block assignments.

Building block 1: Writing a close reading of a specific passage

In the course of the Shakespeare unit, advanced learners will have been collectively performing close readings of scenes and speeches. This first building block requires advanced learners to perform close readings independently. In a unit on *Macbeth*, Macbeth's second full soliloquy (1.7.1–28) is rich for close readings. The students should be expected to write, noticing the minutiae such as the contrast between Macbeth's subjunctive mood ('if it were done' (1)) and the witches' use of the perpetual present tense in an earlier scene ('I'll do, I'll do, and I'll do' (1.3.10)). Advanced learners should be able to recognize and describe how Macbeth has moved from a simple goal – kill the king – to a 'Vaulting ambition' that will not be satisfied (27). Independently, advanced learners should notice that Macbeth describes how good, vulnerable and baby-like Duncan is. There is nothing that can/ will 'spur' Macbeth to kill this good, hospitable king but this 'vaulting ambition' ('full of scorpions is my mind' (3.2.36)). In the first building block, with its limited length and focus, students should be able to both decode and analyse what is in the text and to make coherent links with other parts of the text.

Building block 2: Answering a focused question

Building upon their close reading skills, advanced learners should then be expected to answer an extremely focused question with text-based support. In a unit on *Macbeth*, building block 2 might ask, 'To what extent does Lady Macbeth know what she is capable of doing?' By focusing on the end of Act 1 and the beginning of Act 2, advanced learners will discern a change in Lady Macbeth's understanding of herself and her moral flexibility. While she begins with proclamations about her strength and resolve ('Hie thee hither, / That I may pour my spirits in thine ear' (1.5.25–6) and 'unsex me here, / And fill me, from the crown to the toe, top-full / Of direst cruelty' (1.5.41–3)), she admits that she could not kill Duncan herself because he 'resembled / My father as he slept' (2.2.12–13). The most sophisticated advanced learners might also be able to interpret Lady Macbeth's characterization in light of early modern depictions of Scottish women (see the excerpt from Raphael Holinshed's *Chronicles* above). In other words, advanced learners should be expected to be able to respond to a focused question with a clearly articulated argument that is supported by evidence from the text(s).

Building block 3: Answering a broader question

With an eye toward creating facility with complex texts, teachers can build advanced learners' analytical skills by then asking broader questions of a Shakespeare text. A broader question requires advanced learners to choose evidence from across a specific Shakespeare text (i.e. not simply evidence from one speech or scene). In a unit on *Macbeth*, for instance, advanced learners can write about how *manhood* is discussed and constructed in the play. While many advanced learners will realize that variants on the word *man* are used frequently in the play (e.g. Duncan's first words are 'What bloody man is that?' (1.2.1); and Macbeth and Lady Macbeth have a discussion about what actions 'become a man' (1.7.46)), there are several moments in the play in which characters question if men fear and grieve (e.g. Lady Macbeth claims that Macbeth is 'unmanned in folly' when he fears the ghosts (3.4.72); and Macduff claims that he must 'feel it like a man' when he learns that his wife and children have been killed (4.3.221)). The most sophisticated advanced learners may be able to put the play's construction of manhood in relationship with the play's construction of action (the topic of the speech used in building block 1).

Building block 4: The student-generated question

The final building block asks advanced learners to generate questions that will lead to an argumentative essay of development and length. Advanced

Golda Rosheuvel as Lady Macbeth and Trevor White as Macbeth in the Open Air Theatre Regent's Park 2010 production of Macbeth *re-imagined for everyone aged six and over, directed by Steve Marmion. Photograph by Alastair Muir.*

learners become independent thinkers and writers and gain facility with complex texts through learning to ask and answer good questions. A good question is one that is not too small: asking why Macbeth murders Banquo cannot be answered in an argumentative essay. A good question is one that is not too large: asking how the Gunpowder Plot is evidenced in *Macbeth* cannot be answered in five to six pages. A just-right topic might ask and answer what is the function of Macduff at the end of the play: Malcolm will be king, but Macduff enters with Macbeth's head.

Concluding thoughts

Ultimately, we hope this book enables educators to move their students from an appreciation for Shakespeare to an independent facility with all complex texts. Advanced learners will acquire something more than appreciation from their Shakespeare units when socially collaborative activities are paired with heightened expectations for individual critical analysis. In this way Shakespeare is an excellent vehicle. We believe that learning to analyse a complex text can be pleasurable especially when the method involves twenty-first-century learning habits.

We have little interest in defending Shakespeare in the curriculum based on the cultural capital of his plays or name. Instead we see the works as powerful opportunities to acknowledge and further advance our students' diverse twenty-first-century identities. Without this approach, Shakespeare really will cease to matter in our schools. His plays will be treated as irrelevant matter and dead subjects. The twenty-first-century approach we have outlined provides a way for teachers and advanced learners to continue to explore and challenge the relevance of Shakespeare's works. This is a contest that warrants a collective adventure in the Shakespeare classroom.

BIBLIOGRAPHY

Agamben, Giorgio. *State of Exception*. Trans. Kevin Attell. Chicago: University of Chicago Press, 2005.

Alliance for Inclusion in the Arts. 'Promoting Full Diversity in Theatre, Film and Television'. 20 October 2014. Available online: http://inclusioninthearts.org/

Anderson, Lorin W., and David R. Krathwohl. *A Taxonomy for Learning, Teaching, and Assessing: A Revision of Bloom's Taxonomy of Educational Objectives*. New York: Longman, 2001.

Andrews, John F. 'From the Editor', *Shakespeare Quarterly*, 35 (1984): 515–16.

Appleman, Deborah. *Critical Encounters in High School English: Teaching Literary Theory to Adolescents*. New York: Teachers College Press, 2009.

Atwell, Nancie. *In the Middle: New Understandings About Writing, Reading, and Learning*. Portsmouth, NH: Heinemann Boynton/Cook, 1998.

Austin, J. L. *How to Do Things with Words*. Cambridge: Harvard University Press, 1962.

Badejo, Anita. 'MTV Launches New Campaign to Address "Complicated, Thorny" Race, Gender, and LGBT Issues'. BuzzFeed Entertainment. Available online: http://www.buzzfeed.com/anitabadejo/mtv-launches-new-campaign-to-address-biases#.dlJx4GERB (accessed 30 April 2014).

Banks, Fiona. *Creative Shakespeare: The Globe Education Guide to Practical Shakespeare*. London: Bloomsbury Arden Shakespeare, 2014.

Barlow, Tom. 'Vox Pop: How to Teach Shakespeare at A-Level'. *Teaching Shakespeare 5*, ISSN 2049-3576 (Spring 2014). Available online: http://www.britishshakespeare.ws/wp-content/uploads/2014/01/TS5_WEB2.pdf

Barthelemy, Anthony G. *Black Face, Maligned Race: The Representation of Blacks in English Drama from Shakespeare to Southerne*. Baton Rouge: Louisiana State University Press, 1987.

Beers, Kylene, and Robert E. Probst. *Notice & Note: Strategies for Close Reading*. Portsmouth, NH: Heinemann, 2012.

Bennett, Susan. *Theatre Audiences: A Theory of Production and Reception*. London: Routledge, 1997.

Berry, Barnett and the TeacherSolutions 2030 Team. *Teaching 2030: What We Must Do for Our Students and Our Public Schools: Now and in the Future*. New York: Teachers College Press, 2011.

Berry, Cecily. *The Actor and The Text*. Revised edition. New York: Applause Theatre & Cinema Books, 2000.

Bevington, David, and Gavin Witt. 'Working in workshops', in *Teaching Shakespeare through Performance*, ed. Milla Cozart Riggio (New York: Modern Language Association of America, 1999), 174–89.

Britzman, Deborah P. *Practice Makes Practice: A Critical Study of Learning to Teach*. Albany: State University of New York Press, 2003.

Brustein, Robert. 'Subsidized separatism'. *American Theatre*, 13 (1996): 6.

Bulman, James. *Shakespeare in Performance: The Merchant of Venice*. Manchester: Manchester University Press, 1991.

Burke, Jim. *The English Teacher's Companion: A Completely New Guide to Classroom, Curriculum, and the Profession*. 4th edn. Portsmouth, NH: Heinemann, 2013.

Cohen, Paula Marantz. 'Shylock, My Students, and Me: What I've Learned from 30 Years of Teaching *The Merchant of Venice*', *The American Scholar* (Winter 2010). Available online: https://theamericanscholar.org/shylock-my-students-and-me/

Crowl, Samuel. '"Ocular Proof": Teaching *Othello* in Performance', in *Approaches to Teaching Shakespeare's Othello*, eds. Peter Erickson and Maurice Hunt (New York: The Modern Language Association of America, 2005), 162–8.

Crowther, John, ed. *No Fear Shakespeare: Othello*. New York: SparkNotes, 2003.

Crystal, David. *Pronouncing Shakespeare: The Globe Experiment*. Cambridge: Cambridge University Press, 2005.

Dakin, Mary Ellen. *Reading Shakespeare Film First*. Urbana, IL: National Council of Teachers of English, 2012.

Darling-Hammond, Linda, Peter Ross, and Michael Milliken. 'High School Size, Organization, and Content: What Matters for Student Success?' *Brookings Papers on Education Policy* (2006/7).

Dean, Deborah. *Genre Theory: Teaching, Writing, and Being*. Urbana, IL: National Council of Teachers of English, 2008.

Dede, Chris. 'Comparing Frameworks for 21st Century Skills', in *21st Century Skills: Rethinking How Students Learn*, eds James A. Bellanca and Ronald S. Brandt (Bloomington, IN: Solution Tree Press, 2010), 55–71.

Drakakis, John. 'Introduction'. *The Merchant of Venice*. The Arden Shakespeare Third Series. London: Bloomsbury Arden Shakespeare, 2011.

Edmiston, Brian. *Transforming Teaching and Learning with Active and Dramatic Approaches: Engaging Students Across the Curriculum*. Abingdon, Oxon; New York: Routledge, 2013.

Edmiston, Brian, Jill Sampson, and Jessica Sharp. '100 Ways to Teach Shakespeare in Middle and High School: Teaching Shakespeare like Actors, Directors, Audiences and Designers'. Workshop presented at the National Council of Teachers of English national conference, Las Vegas, November 2012.

Elements of Literature, 3rd Course. Bel Air, CA: Holt, Reinhart and Winston, 2007.

Esquith, Rafe. Phone Interview with Ayanna Thompson. 10 November 2009. Published with permission.

Esquith, Rafe. *There Are No Shortcuts*. New York: Pantheon Books, 2003.

Ewbank, Inga-Stina, 'The Tragedy of Macbeth: A Genetic Text', in *Thomas Middleton: The Collected Work*, eds. Gary Taylor and John Lavagnino (Oxford: Clarendon Press, 2007).

Faiola, Anthony, and Souad Mekhennet. 'Denmark Tries a Soft-handed Approach to Returned Islamist Fighters', *The Washington Post*,

19 October 2014. Available online: http://www.washingtonpost.com/
world/europe/denmark-tries-a-soft-handed-approach-to-returned-islamist-
fighters/2014/10/19/3516e8f3-515e-4adc-a2cb-c0261dd7dd4a_story.html

Faiola, Anthony, and Souad Mekhennet. 'Aarhus: The Danish Town Where Syria's
Jihadist Fighters are Welcomed Home', *The Independent*, 20 October 2014.
Available online: http://www.independent.co.uk/news/world/europe/aarhus-the-
danish-town-where-syrias-fighters-are-welcomed-home-9806876.html

Folger Shakespeare Library. 'Lesson 15: Tear Him for His Bad Verses: Cinna the
Poet and Shakespeare's Sonnets'. n.d. Available online: http://www.folger.edu/
eduLePlanDtl.cfm?lpid=781

Gee, James Paul. 'Affinity Space: From Age of Mythology to Today's Schools',
James Paul Gee, 6 June 2009. Available online: http://www.jamespaulgee.com/
node/5

Gee, James Paul. *What Video Games Have to Teach Us about Learning and
Literacy*. New York: Palgrave Macmillan, 2003.

Gibson, Rex. *Teaching Shakespeare*. Cambridge: Cambridge University Press,
1998.

Gonzalez, Norma, and Luis Moll. 'Cruzando el Puente: Building Bridges to Funds
of Knowledge', *Educational Policy*, 16 (2002): 623–41.

Hattie, John. *Visible Learning for Teachers: Maximizing Impact on Learning*.
London: Routledge, 2011.

Hillocks, George. 'Forward', in *Transforming Talk into Text: Argument Writing,
Inquiry, and Discussion, Grades 6-12*, ed. Thomas M. McCann (New York:
Teacher's College Press, 2014).

Holinshed, Raphael. 'Chronicles of England, Scotland and Ireland (1587)', in *The
Arden Shakespeare Macbeth*, ed. Kenneth Muir (London: Bloomsbury Arden
Shakespeare, 1984).

Hooper, Simon. 'Denmark Introduces Rehab for Syrian Fighters', *Al Jazeera*, 7
September 2014. Available online: http://www.aljazeera.com/indepth/
features/2014/09/denmark-introduces-rehab-syrian-fighters-
201496125229948625.html

Hunter, Robin, and Madeline C. Hunter. *Madeline Hunter's Mastery Teaching:
Increasing Instructional Effectiveness in Elementary and Secondary Schools*.
Thousand Oaks, CA: Corwin Press, 2004.

Jago, Carol. *Papers, Papers, Papers: An English Teacher's Survival Guide*.
Portsmouth, NH: Heinemann, 2005.

Jenkins, Henry. 'Confronting the Challenges of Participatory Culture: Media
Education for the 21st Century (Part One)'. *Confessions of an ACA-Fan: The
Official Weblog of Henry Jenkins*. 20 October 2006. Available online: http://
henryjenkins.org/2006/10/confronting_the_challenges_of.html

Jenkins, Henry, and Wyn Kelley. *Reading in a Participatory Culture: Remixing
Moby-Dick in the English Classroom*. New York: Teachers College Press, 2013.

Jenkins, Henry, with Ravi Purushotma, Margaret Weigel, Katie Clinton, and
Alice J. Robison. *Confronting the Challenges of Participatory Culture: Media
Education for the 21st Century*. Cambridge, MA: MIT Press, 2009.

Kennedy, Dennis. *Looking at Shakespeare: A Visual History of Twentieth-Century
Performance*. Cambridge: Cambridge University Press, 1993.

King James. *Daemonologie and News from Scotland* (1597), in *The Demonology
of King James 1*, ed. Donald Tyson (Woodbury: Llewellyn Publications, 2011.)

Lave, Jean, and Etienne Wenger. *Situated Learning: Legitimate Peripheral Participation*. Cambridge: Cambridge University Press, 1991.

Markus, Zoltan. 'Der Merchant von Velence: *The Merchant of Venice* in London, Berlin, and Budapest during World War II', in *Shakespeare and European Politics*, eds Dirk Delabastita, Jozef De Vos, and Paul J. C. M. Franssen (Newark: University of Delaware Press, 2008.)

McKinnon, James. 'Creative Copying?: The Pedagogy of Adaptation', *Canadian Theater Review*, 147 (2011): 55–60.

Metzger, Mary. 'Shakespeare for a New Age', *The English Journal*, 92 (2002): 22–8.

Miazga, Mark. 'Shakespeare and the (Common Core) Assessments'. NCTE 2014 Annual Convention: Story as the Landscape of Knowing. National Harbor, Washington DC. 21 November 2014. Conference Presentation.

'Moor, n.2'. *OED Online*. Oxford University Press, December 2014. Available online: http://www.oed.com/view/Entry/121965?rskey=0OkTB5&result=2&isAdvanced=false#eid

MTV Strategic Insights and David Binder Research, 'DBR MTV Bias Survey Executive Summary.' 4–9 April 2014. Available online: http://cdn.lookdifferent.org/content/studies/000/000/001/DBR_MTV_Bias_Survey_Executive_Summary.pdf.

MTV Strategic Insights and David Binder Research. 'MTV Bias Survey II Final Results'. 4–9 April 2014. Available online: http://cdn.lookdifferent.org/content/studies/000/000/003/DBR_MTV_Bias_Survey_Full_Report_II.pdf?1398858309

National Center for Social Research. 'British Social Attitudes'. NATCEN Social Research that Works for Society. NatCen. Available online: http://www.natcen.ac.uk/our-research/research/british-social-attitudes/

Neelands, Jonothan. 'Acting Together: Ensemble as a Democratic Process in Art and Life', *Research in Drama Education*, 14 (2009): 173–89.

Noble, Louise. 'The Fille Vierge as Pharmakon: The Therapeutic Value of Desdemona's Corpse', in *Disease, Diagnosis, and Cure on the Early Modern State*, eds Stephanie Moss and Kaara Peterson. (Aldershot: Ashgate, 2004), 135–50.

Noden, Harry. *Image Grammar, Second Edition: Teaching Grammar as Part of the Writing Process*. Portsmouth, NH: Heinemann, 2011.

O'Brien, Peggy. *Shakespeare Set Free: Teaching A Midsummer Night's Dream, Romeo and Juliet, and Macbeth*. New York: Simon and Shuster, 2006.

Omi, Michael, and Howard Winant. *Racial Formation in the United States: From the 1960s to the 1990s*. New York: Routledge, 1994.

Oregon Shakespeare Festival Audience Surveys. Ashland, OR: OSF Archives.

Orgel, Stephen. *The Authentic Shakespeare: And Other Problems of the Early Modern Stage*. New York and London: Routledge, 2002.

Orgel, Stephen. *Imagining Shakespeare: A History of Texts and Visions*. Basingstoke: Palgrave Macmillan, 2003.

Oz, Avraham. 'The Merchant of Venice in Israel', in *Foreign Shakespeare*, ed. Dennis Kennedy (Cambridge: Cambridge University Press, 1993.)

Palfrey, Simon, and Tiffany Stern. *Shakespeare in Parts*. Oxford: Oxford University Press, 2011.

Pike, Mark. *Teaching Secondary English*. London: Paul Chapman Publishing Sage, 2004.

Popham, W. James. *Transformative Assessment in Action: An Inside Look at Applying the Process*. Alexandria, VA: ASCD, 2011.

Rokison, Abigail. *Shakespeare for Young People: Productions, Versions and Adaptations*. London: Bloomsbury Arden Shakespeare, 2013.

Romano, Tom. *Clearing the Way: Working with Teenage Writers*. Portsmouth, NH: Heinemann, 1987.

Rosenblatt, Louise M. *The Reader, the Text, the Poem: The Transactional Theory of the Literary Work*. Carbondale: Southern Illinois University Press, 1994.

Royal Shakespeare Company. *Stand Up for Shakespeare: A Manifesto for Shakespeare in Schools*, 3. Available online: https://www.rsc.org.uk/downloads/stand-up-for-shakespeare-manifesto.pdf

Royal Shakespeare Company. 'What is Teaching Shakespeare?' n.d. *Teaching Shakespeare*. Available online: http://www.teachingshakespeare.ac.uk/about.aspx

Sabatino, Lindsay. 'Improving Writing Literacies through Digital Gaming Literacies: Facebook Gaming in the Composition Classroom', *Computers and Composition*, (June 2014): 41–53.

Scot, Reginald. *The Discoverie of Witchcraft* (1584). New York: Dover Publications, 1972.

Second City Network. 'Sassy Gay Friend – Romeo and Juliet'. *YouTube*. Available online: https://www.youtube.com/watch?v=lwnFE_NpMsE

Shannon, Laurie. *The Accommodated Animal: Cosmopolity in Shakespearean Locales*. Chicago: University of Chicago Press, 2013.

Simon, John. 'We close in Verona'. *New York Magazine*. 6 June 1988.

Steele, Claude. 'A Threat in the Air: How Stereotypes Shape Intellectual Performance and Identity', *The American Psychologist*, 52 (1997): 613–29.

Steele, Claude. *Whistling Vivaldi: And Other Clues to How Stereotypes Affect Us*. New York: W. W. Norton & Company, 2010.

Steier, Eli. 'Re: Merchant of Venice'. NING. Ning Mode Media. 4 October 2010.

Stredder, James. *The North Face of Shakespeare: Activities for Teaching the Plays*. Cambridge: Cambridge University Press, 2009.

Sturgess, Kim C. *Shakespeare and the American Nation*. Cambridge: Cambridge University Press, 2004.

Tatum, Beverly D. *'Why Are All the Black Kids Sitting Together in the Cafeteria?' and Other Conversations About Race*. New York: Basic Books, 2003.

Taylor, Matthew, and Hugh Muir. 'Racism on the Rise in Britain', *The Guardian Weekly*, 27 May 2014.

Thompson, Ayanna, 'What is a "Weyward" *Macbeth*?', in *Weyward Macbeth: Intersections of Race and Performance*, eds Scott Newstok and Ayanna Thompson (New York: Palgrave Macmillan, 2010), 3–10.

Thompson, Ayanna. *Passing Strange: Shakespeare, Race, and Contemporary America*. Oxford: Oxford University Press 2011.

Traub, Valerie, ed. *The Oxford Handbook for Shakespeare and Embodiment*. Oxford: Oxford University Press, (forthcoming).

Turchi, Peter. *A Muse and a Maze: Writing as Puzzle, Mystery, and Magic*. San Antonio, TX: Trinity University Press, 2014.

Tynes, Brendesha M. and Suzanne L. Markoe. 'The Role of Color-Blind Racial Attitudes in Reactions to Racial Discrimination on Social Network Sites', *Journal of Diversity in Higher Education*, 3 (2010): 1–13.

Vygotsky, Lev. *Mind in Society: The Development of Higher Psychological Processes*. Cambridge: Harvard University Press, 1980.

Woolnough, Peter. 'Catering for an Assessment-Driven Curriculum', in *Teaching English: Developing as a Reflective Secondary Teacher*, eds Alyson Midgley, Peter Woolnough, Lynne Warham, Phil Rigby and Carol Evans (London: Sage Publications Limited, 2009), 140–63.

INDEX